THE COMPLETE SERAPHIN MESSAGES

TEN YEARS OF
TELEPATHIC COMMUNICATION
WITH AN ANGEL

Volume 5: Messages 431 – 450

SERAPHIN'S QUESTION AND ANSWER SESSION
on relationships, world problems, spiritual progress,
health, the future and the unseen

Rosie Jackson

**THIS BOOK IS DEDICATED
TO ALL READERS
AND ALL THOSE WHO SEEK ANSWERS**

May you be blessed with

intense curiosity,
deep compassion,
the desire to overcome all obstacles,
and the thirst to fully understand

for these will move you forward on your spiritual path,
enabling you to contribute to the
rebuilding of a new world

My deepest gratitude goes to Seraphin
for his trust and for the wisdom he has provided

Deep gratitude also to all the spiritual seekers
who have shared their stories and posed their questions in
Seraphin's question and answer session.

Thank you to all translators, proof-readers and video makers
for their dedication to the Seraphin material

Rosie Jackson

Bibliografische Information der Deutschen Nationalbibliothek:
Die Deutsche Nationalbibliothek verzeichnet diese Publikation in der
Deutschen Nationalbibliografie; detaillierte bibliografische Daten sind
im Internet über http://dnb.dnb.de abrufbar.

Herstellung und Verlag: BoD – Books on Demand, Norderstedt

Erste Auflage Juni 2021

ISBN: 9783753444741

TABLE OF CONTENTS

SERAPHIN ANSWERS QUESTIONS ON RELATIONSHIPS

SERAPHIN ANSWERS QUESTIONS ON BEHAVIOUR

SERAPHIN ANSWERS QUESTIONS ON THE UNSEEN

SERAPHIN ANSWERS QUESTIONS ABOUT THE FUTURE

INTRODUCTION

For over a decade, I have been receiving telepathic messages from the angel Seraphin in the form of very fast medial writing, noting down the words which I hear in my mind. This is the fifth volume of *The Complete Seraphin Messages*, and consists of two parts.

Part One contains Seraphin's most recent messages, received between November 2020 and May 2021 - a period of intense physical restriction due to "pandemic" measures, and thus also of intense soul-searching.

Seraphin makes it clear to us that nothing is going to "return to normal" following the lifting of these restrictions. In these twenty most recent messages, Seraphin addresses us in an increasingly acute situation – a world permeated with corruption, uncertainty, violence and confusion, and he asks us whether, in the face of this, we are EXPRESSING THE DIVINE IN EVERY MOMENT, or whether this is something we only do on Sundays.

Why is this so important?

Seraphin is very clear about this:

"Your actions, if they are guided by the DIVINE WITHIN.
are the "guiding lights" which will rally society
when it reaches its deepest collective trauma"

Seraphin urges us to act, for the sake of humanity:

"If you fall into desperation, how can you be effective? If you look away, how can you reasonably assess what is in front of you? And if you fear, how can you lead the "sheep" into the fold?"

He also advises "absolute singlemindedness of purpose", without succumbing to any distractions. This is one of Seraphin's most astounding statements from this volume:

"If you know 100 percent that you are walking in the right
direction, and if you know 100 percent that you are
benefitting humanity with every footstep and every breath,
then you will be happy always"

This is a "test" on many levels, in completely different ways which meet the eye. Either we have blithely accepted the proffered narrative, or we have searched for our own truth. In our comparative isolation, we have also been forced to reconsider our priorities, what we are living for, what has genuine lasting value, and what constitutes "happiness". We have also learnt about our dependencies, our addictions, our measure of willingness to comply and our measure of determination to resist.

Our greatest challenge is that we are often anchored in the material world, falling into despair when this fails to function, and failing to recognize THE GREAT UNSEEN, and here I would like to refer you to a really stunning message in this volume: Seraphin Message 449: The Great Unseen.

Part Two of this volume consists of a question and answer session during which I channelled Seraphin's answers to 92 questions, posed by spiritual seekers on a public internet forum in 2016.

What questions do people have?

What answers does Seraphin give?

The questions cover a wide range of subjects and acute problems. Usually, the answers contain valuable advice and a huge expansion of perspectives which the questioner can "run with", if so desired. Often, the questioners felt completely exhilarated after receiving their reply, because it gave them so many new aspects to think about.

Seraphin's answers are not "cut and dried". He will never answer "yes" or "no". He will never hand out solutions on a plate, with no personal effort involved. This is out of love. This is due to his eternal desire to support us in our spiritual progress, to make us into independent thinkers who will launch joyfully into new investigations of self, of our behaviour, of our relationships with others.

Seraphin wants us to conduct our own investigations and come to our own enlightened conclusions. He is less of a teacher of concrete knowledge and more of a catalyst in service to our spiritual growth.

Seraphin's answers are always laced with great compassion. He offers solace to those who need it. He chooses exactly the right words to communicate with the individual concerned, and provides exactly the right level of information so that it can be fully digested.

While the numbered messages (450 to date) which are addressed to all inhabitants of earth have their own intrinsic value, striking different chords with different readers, the incredible gift of such a question and answer session is to receive tailor-made, customised answers which never fail to address individual questioners in a way which they can currently accept. It also serves as inspiration for readers, demonstrating that it is possible to build a relationship with one's own personal unseen guide.

Seraphin never fails to thank these seekers of his wisdom, and he always reminds them of their intrinsic value and huge potential which will benefit humanity if they launch into their various missions with enthusiasm, dedication and determination.

To Seraphin, my eternal gratitude.

Rosie Jackson, June 2021

Seraphin Message 431: FIREWORKS IN THE DISTANCE
Through Rosie. 12th November 2020

Dear Citizens of Earth; we assume that if you are reading this, you have a certain measure of concern about present "despiralling" events and the state of your earth. We use the word "despiralling" as in the image of a whirlpool sucking everything down into a bottomless pit.

More and more cases of criminality are arising, especially on the political scene where there is a great battle for power, and indeed those who have committed these crimes will inevitably be sucked towards their "doom". Escape is unavoidable. Their actions have determined the results, and this is the way the cosmic law of cause and effect pans out.

Can you see that a ribbon of tension is building up to such an intensity that your earth will be strangled by the EFFECTS of violence and corruption – not only the violence of present times, but also the CUMULATIVE EFFECT OF ALL WARS IN THE PAST, involving the slaughter of millions on various parts of the globe at various stages of your history?

Does your heart go out to her, the witness of so much suffering, traumatized by it, unable to put an end to it, seeing the aftermath – the physical, mental and spiritual destruction? Would you not also say I CANNOT TAKE IT ANY MORE?

And we say that all physical demise leaves its mark and is accompanied by spiritual death, as everything is intimately connected. Your planet can no longer play host to masses of evil-minded people. YES, EVIL – not simply careless or absent-minded. It has been one of your core faults to fail to recognise evil, thus allowing it full reign, thus allowing it to become rampant worldwide. What is the remedy for this? What will create mass awakening to this situation?

Can the earth shoulder it alone? Are you alone in the universe? Are there no other forces observing your sorry plight? Is no-one willing to help? You can be sure that the answer to all these questions is NO.

Let us return to the title of this piece, which announces that there will be "fireworks in the distance". There will be some who are cowering in fear and who will hide in their homes. There will be others who hear the noise and see a dull light on the horizon. There will be yet others who will run to the nearest hill to get a better view. And some of these may even have the presence of mind to take binoculars with them to see them better.

From a height, they will clearly see the "fireworks". It will be a spectacular view. There will be multiple explosions. They will be struck with awe, wondering what on earth is going on. Those who have more extended knowledge will know that this massive release of "energy" and "show and tell" involves great elements of danger. They will also know that it simultaneously means that the world is becoming safer.

Those who intuitively know that this is the beginning of a new era will simultaneously know that this means the death of the "old", and that these "fireworks" do not simply symbolize celebration, but mark the end of a way of life, a way of thinking and a way of behaving.

Thus, there will be a global party and a global funeral, accompanied by a loud explosion of firecrackers as is the custom in some Asian funerals.

Where are you in all this, Beloveds? Our messages have tried to prepare you. May you fare well in this next phase. Seraphin.

Seraphin Message 432:
EXPECT COLOURS WHERE THEY ARE NOT
Through Rosie. 15th November 2020

Can you imagine,
Beloved Humans on Earth,
that you are deeply loved?

Can you imagine that there is a vast host of (for you) unseen beings who are continuing – at all times of the day and night – to usher you into directions which spur your growth, to make you more resilient to any "tragedies", to increase your serenity and courage in the face of all dangers, to provide signs for you to follow along a path which is purely spiritual in nature and – if followed – will lead you to a place of perfect poise and balance?

Can you imagine that this is the same for each individual, providing that they have a morsel of conscience to which one can appeal? Can you conceive of this massive orchestration instigated and maintained by the helpers of DIVINE HAND? Can you imagine that you are THAT IMPORTANT and that you can rise to such DIVINE HEIGHTS?

We say that this is not only possible,
but actually PROGRAMMED FOR YOU.

And can you imagine that all DIVINE PROGRAMMING
is different for each individual?

And can you imagine that any alternative force, however devious, cunning, unrelenting and determined, can never succeed – in the final analysis - to infest this DIVINE PROGRAMMING?

From our point of view, as we observe the increasing drama and trauma developing on your planet resulting from the actions of those who defy the DIVINE, and resulting from the actions of those who IGNORE DIVINE SIGNS, you are but taking small deviations on a road already given, a war already won.

But to you, it may seem that your planet is nearing extinction, fraught with war and now also with a so-called virus which threatens to bring everything to a standstill. But this is merely a hiccup in a long journey upwards, in the sense of spiritual development which stretches eternally through many lives and experiences.

With this message, we do not intend to belittle you, caught as you are in present fears and seemingly threatening circumstances, but to remind you of your GREATER SELVES which you cannot see in their entirety.

Your actions on earth are just one aspect of your
MULTI-COLOURED AND MULTI-FACETTED PERSONALITY
which has descended to earth for a new adventure of
HOW TO RETURN TO DIVINE BEHAVIOUR.

So, though your horizon may presently be restricted, know that there is SO MUCH MORE, and that the more you strive to see, the more your life will turn from black and white monotony into fully-fledged, multi-coloured perspectives.

It is fear, as in a main cause, which presents you from expanding your horizons.

Dare to look.

Dare to expect colours where there are presently not, and hold this bright vision in your hearts, Beloveds, when you find yourselves travelling through this temporary darkness.

We love you as always, Seraphin

Seraphin Message 433: EXPRESSING THE DIVINE
Through Rosie, 19th November 2020

Which part of yourselves are you expressing, Beloveds?

Is it the coarse, worldly part of yourselves which you present to a harsh and unrelenting world? Is it the fearful, intimidated parts of yourselves which is your only perceived answer to atrocities around you? Is it the ego-driven part of yourselves which dives recklessly into the crowd as soon as you move into the public arena? Are you continuously on a stage, defending your position, or making "waves" in a desperate attempt to be seen? Are you exposing the traumatized parts of yourself, presenting yourself as a victim, to make others feel guilty without giving them a chance to understand? Are you indulging in "unsacred" activities, thus contributing to a less than holy world? Or is there a wondrous, secret, creative part of yourselves which is begging to be brought out into the open, if only you would grasp the courage?

Self-expression may be all very well if it alleviates pain, but does it increase another's pain? Is it possible to "go within" and search out that which makes you unique and to promulgate this part of yourself as an INSPIRATION for others?

You will note that our foremost form of connecting with you in this message is questioning, as a way of instigating new thought processes and so that you have another opportunity to self-assess, and to assess the QUALITY of what you are putting out into the world. Is your output beneficial to you only, or to others also? Does it increase further division of your society (and we say that you are on the verge of final division into multiple, militarized factions which are all too ready to throw themselves at each other's throats in their "passion" for their own particular agenda) or does your output increase understanding, heal wounds and create peace?

All this we would put before you as you decide where to place your energy, and how to present your particular truth to the world.

Note that this is ONLY YOUR PARTICULAR TRUTH, and that while it is important to communicate this, it should not take on belligerent forms which serve only to shock others and to make them turn away in fear or disgust. Earth is riddled with those whose perspectives do not go beyond the perimeters of their own existence, their own procedures and their own trauma. We are not saying that trauma should not be voiced or treated (and indeed the great majority of earth's citizens have been exposed to some manner of traumatic experiences). We are saying that it is necessary to treat these primarily in a private framework, increasing personal understanding of yourselves, before you present the public with a "half-baked" issue or incomplete story.

This may sound extremely harsh to many, especially those involved in lobbies for the oppressed. We admire your courage, but we do not condone violent methods. And you must approach your audience in a way that they are predisposed to understand. Otherwise, your efforts are useless.

How often do you express the "Divine", thus uplifting and inspiring your fellow humans? Do you do this once a week, when you are in a heightened mood after a Sunday service or favourite pastime? Do you do this on special days like birthdays, or do you express the Divine part of yourselves every day and in every moment? We leave it to you to answer these questions. Know that your answer, and your subsequent actions - if they are guided by the DIVINE WITHIN - are the "guiding lights" which will rally society when it reaches its deepest collective trauma.

This is still to come, Beloveds.
Therefore we ask you to make ready.
Seraphin.

Seraphin Message 434: BREAKING INTO A RUN
Through Rosie. 26th November 2020

Citizens of Earth who are moving – whether you are aware or unaware – towards a serious set of "crossroads".

At the moment, you are still pacing rather casually. Some of you are extremely cautious, due to restrictive measures in place, or due to anxiety because you realise that many things have been going very wrong, and you sense that the revelation of the truth will actually be so much more devastating than expected. In this, you will be right.

And so, there you walk, either blind, or blinded by some sort of naïve belief that everything is alright, or with downright disinterest, or with a sense of dreadful foreboding, but all knowing that there is NO GOING BACK, and that it is NOT POSSIBLE TO STOP, and that it is not possible to

START OVER WITH A CLEAN PLATE,
BECAUSE ALL STORIES
AND ALL IMPLEMENTED "SOURCES"
MUST PROGRESS TO THEIR
INEVITABLE CONCLUSIONS AND RESULTS.

As intensity picks up, you will stop walking and you will break into a run. You will have to WATCH YOUR STEP CAREFULLY, AND YOU WILL HAVE TO BECOME INTENSELY AWARE OF YOUR SURROUNDINGS, OTHERWISE YOU WILL FALL BY THE WAYSIDE, and this is definitely not your mandate.

With this short message, we would like to warn you that it is time to sharpen your senses and to attune yourselves even more to the advice you receive from within, for this will PREVENT YOUR FALL whenever there is danger of fatigue, shock or desperation.

YOU MUST KEEP GOING, ONE STEP AT A TIME, with concentration and dedication to the cause, which is of course the WILL OF THE DIVINE, and which is of course to bring about BALANCE AND SERENITY THROUGH YOUR BEHAVIOUR.

If you fall into desperation, how can you be effective? If you look away, how can you reasonably assess what is in front of you? And if you fear, how can you lead the "sheep" into the fold?

Do you even know where the fold is, or what will comfort those who suffer?

Develop your personal strategies, Beloveds, for you will be "on call", and there will be enough who need your help. Seraphin.

Seraphin Message 435:
MOVING TO HIGHER HEART GROUND
Through Rosie. 7th December 2020

Have you noticed, Citizens of Earth, that you are being subtly or even blatantly pushed towards higher moral ground?

There is a powerful "undercurrent" forcing you to pause, to turn around, to survey the plains behind you which are choked in mud and slime, smothering all growth, and to critically appraise the source of all this. It is not enough to simply lift yourselves out of this morass, to escape the dregs and to move to the sides, waiting and hoping that the sun will come out and dry it all up, burning the dross away.

Hope alone will change nothing. Your action is required, movement is required – and by this we mean INNER MOVEMENT TO HIGHER MORAL GROUND, for lack of this has caused the problems under which the majority of humankind presently suffer. Yourself included.

This may involve adopting a series of "absolute" or (in some eyes) radical behaviours, as in keeping to one's own course without any deviation. This is a position of absolute clarity and absolute confidence that you are following the path which is destined for you, and the path which you are simultaneously CREATING FOR YOURSELF.

It is all very well to hesitate and take breaks, wondering whether another direction or approach is better. It is all very well to take a "holiday" from the strenuous nature of such a journey. It is all very well to say "being strict is not the best way".

However, absolute singlemindedness of purpose will serve you best, bringing you swiftly to a place of extremely valuable experience and knowledge which you are then capable of transmitting to others in the most effective way. Suffice to say that your self-discipline in following such steps is ultimately for the good of others, and therefore for yourself, as the greatest joy is to help others on their way.

This may sound like working under extreme duress. We say that if you know 100 percent that you are walking in the right direction, and if you know 100 percent that you are benefitting humanity with every footstep and every breath, then you will be happy always. You will also know exactly how much rest is necessary to replenish yourself, so that you can continue on this journey in the optimal manner. Thus, there will be no such thing as "stress" or "burn out", only continuous joy.

So what direction should you take?

Many on your planet are dictated by needs – the need to eat, have shelter and a supportive community. Money is still (but not for ever) the great dictator. It dictates what you choose to do for a living, it dictates your school and career choices, even your friendships and marriage alliances. You may be able to free yourselves from the dictates of financial concerns for a while, but ultimately, they are always hovering in the background.

With the upcoming great changes, which include the "falling away" of many so-called jobs, the money aspect will retreat into the background, and that which is truly valuable will be revealed in full clarity, which is cooperation on an unprecedented scale in all areas of life. The "dictator" in this new setting will be compassion. Situations which you cannot yet imagine will raise their heads, and you will be challenged to react. May the heart be your compass now and in the future.

How many people do you hate at the moment? Can you open your heart to them? Do you rail daily against those who – in your opinion – do not understand, are acting in a crazy way, are succumbing to fear, are reacting violently or are hiding from their responsibilities? Was there a time when you did exactly the same?

Are you a paragon? If you think you are, and if you think you know the answers to all questions, think again, for if you are perfect, there would be nothing more to learn: yet you are on this planet STILL, and you have not completed your LEARNING PROCESSES: otherwise, you would already have moved on.

Remember that there is so much about other people, and their journey, that you do not know, and it is not your mandate to pass judgement, but to get to know them much better SO THAT YOU UNDERSTAND THEM.

Let not this arrogant stance separate you from your brothers and sisters who are still struggling along their very difficult paths. Do not complain in loud, belligerent voices about all the detrimental activities of others, RATHER SET OUT FOR HIGHER GROUND YOURSELF, COMPASSED BY THE HEART.

May your compassion expand to include ALL, just as you yourself have been included in the past – or in past lives – by beings of a higher spiritual nature who have sought to help and accompanying you through the "valley of death". Yes, these are strong words, yet the "valley of death" – a narrow path through which all shall necessarily pass – is approaching, and we urge you to guide and hold the hands of those who require assistance. Seraphin.

Seraphin Message 436:
YOUR CHOICE OF HOPE OR CONVICTION
Through Rosie, 30th December 2020

Have you very little hope left, Citizens of Earth?

And if you do still hope, what is your assessment of the effects which "hoping" will achieve? Many will – in the face of adversity – simply sit back and "hope for the best". This is placing hope in people and events OUTSIDE OF YOURSELVES, abdicating responsibility and allowing others to aspire to whatever you are yourself aspiring.

This is a sort of transfer of emotion, and also – unwittingly – a transfer of power, for you cannot assume that others share your particular intentions.

When will you awake to this power which you are giving away to others? To hope, without taking action, is futile. It is like burying your face in your hands and resigning yourself to fate. This sort of behaviour is extremely detrimental, allowing everyone else to determine where your path will take you. THOSE WHO DO NOT HOPE BUT WHO GO INTO ACTON WILL TAKE OVER.

You can hope, of course, that they have good intentions, yet in the world as it presently stands, with increasing corruption bubbling to the surface, this would be a very naïve assumption.

To believe in the "good" in people is all very well, and it will on occasion be justified, yet you must realise that there is a very malevolent strain in your human society which is dragging you all downhill and which is not working for the general good. Instead, these people are harnessing your energy to further their own power.

If you hope, it sounds like you are not convinced. It indicates that your thoughts are not grounded in solid facts - in certain knowing, or in conviction that one step leads to another, and that you can in effect put these steps into motion.

Motion is the focus here. To simply hope is too faint a signal to disperse evil. You must become a VERY BRIGHT LIGHT TO BURN AWAY THE FOG, just as the sun burns away the mist on a sunny morning.

You are riding on the edge of history, beloved citizens of earth: you are not residing in your armchairs on a cosy evening. You are PIVOTAL in what happens next. IT IS YOUR GOALS WHICH DETERMINE THE FUTURE.

In these turbulent times where you may be reduced to fear and where you may tend to want to hunker down and distract yourselves from all the events you cannot understand, the bell will ring and there will be a loud knock at the door.

You will suddenly be hit by icy winds and the postman will present you with your "bills" – your reckonings – as well as what you ordered (the results of your actions) and – if you are lucky – your love letters (which will of course be the result of the love you have bestowed at an earlier date).

In short, you will feel the effects of your behaviour, and if your behaviour has been negative, the results will be negative or without substance (in the case of those who hope only).

So how can you become convinced?

If you examine these effects carefully, you will be able to trace them to what you have done in the past. You will see the inseparable connection. This will spur you on to set the ball rolling in a positive direction, with much more effort than simply "hoping", so that you AND ALL OTHERS can receive the positive effects of your chosen course.

This message is just another way of saying HOW IMPORTANT YOU ARE and DO NOT GET LOST IN THE OVERWHELM of what is presently happening.

The situation is intense – the moment before the big dipper carriages start to rush downhill at immense speed – and we anticipate that many will not be able to remain calm and centred in the rush that ensues.

If you are intensely aware of your own creative power, you will never need to feel helpless, irrespective of the rapid pace and the whirlwind of events unfurling around you. Thus, be the eye in the storm. Act with dignity and presence so that you can better direct those who are floundering. Thus we leave you today, Seraphin

Seraphin Message 437:
LIBERATION FROM SOUL CAGES TO SOUL CASES
Through Rosie, 11th January 2021

Many of you can be partially excused, Children of Earth, for not knowing what freedom really is. You will chant it at demonstrations, you will feel the breath of freedom as you stand at the top of a mountain looking at a panorama of stunning countryside, you will even perhaps jump off such a pinnacle in a parachute or free fall from a plane in order to experience the "freedom of flying", yet what you are actually experiencing is a "rush of adrenalin" or protest in an otherwise perhaps uninteresting or cramped existence. Think also of the many millions who live in cramped, unsanitary circumstances with little nourishment, and to whom the word "freedom" would mean something completely different, such as being free of hunger or free of disease.

But of course, there are also even greater scenarios which many of you cannot conceive of: that this is a PRISON PLANET, surrounded for thousands of years by protective "fences" – not to protect you, but to protect the negative energies of you from seeping into the rest of the cosmos.

Of this prison, you have not been aware.

Your world of serfs and underlings largely acting in accordance with the wishes and commands (whether seen or unseen) or your slave masters, is also a battle taking place, largely without you being aware of it.

You are similarly unaware of the larger consequences, or of your position as a planet in an area of system rebellion.

Your area of "space", as you would call it, has long since separated itself from DIVINE ALLEGIANCES, and so you have been quarantined and given the chance to sort yourselves out internally – fighting it out amongst yourselves without tainting your planetary neighbours (yes, they exist in bountiful number, again, far from your awareness).

This quarantine situation (and maybe some of you will listen up more, now that you are more aware of what life in quarantine is, due to your "covid" situation) has meant that – irrespective of what you call "death" – you are CAGED IN ONE PLACE, allowed to incarnate ONLY HERE.

This was intended as a period of reprieve, for you to find your feet in an enclosed environment, fighting it out, being confronted with the intense "darkness" of yourselves in order to be able to TURN AROUND AND DO THE OPPOSITE.

It was an experiment to encourage much BETTER BEHAVIOUR THAN BEFORE. In some case, this has been achieved. With the majority, it has not, and your spiritual progression has been extremely slow.

This is what life is about, Children of Earth:
SPIRITUAL PROGRESSION

And we of the celestial realms will always act to further this, in whatever way we deem to be possible and in alignment with COSMIC LAW.

However. All experiments come to an end, and it is time for the effects of Lucifer – the prime mover in this scenario – to be shattered into tiny smithereens.

There are those who have learnt, and there are those who have not learnt anything. Their behaviour is still on the same barbaric, heinous level as long ago, despite their perhaps refined and commanding appearance.

Always remember that cosmic law will kick in at exactly the right time, and be sure that this is coming to you, wayward ones on earth.

To those who have been forced to take part in this experiment, and who have increased the quality of their behaviour and who have realized that their greatest joy is serving others, YOU WILL BE RELEASED FROM YOUR CAGES.

Each of them – as a soul – is then
FREE TO MOVE ON AS DESIRED.

Their "soul" will no longer be forced to incarnate on earth.
They may choose their own "casing" or "vehicle"
for their next experience.

They will have FREEDOM OF CHOICE.

Those who have not changed, and who refuse to submit
to cosmic law, will ENTER A NEW CAGE.

For each "soul" presently living on earth, the experience which is to come will differ, but you can be sure that the future you experience will DEPEND ON YOUR PARTICULAR MERITS.

As this time draws ever closer, we ask you to reflect on what freedom actually means to you, and whether imposing restrictions is sometimes necessary in order to awaken. This has been the story of earth.

We will welcome you into our arms when the cage falls.

Seraphin.

Seraphin Message 438:
THE GREAT THAW AND THE SOUND OF SNOW MELTING
Through Rosie, 11th January 2021

You will only hear the sound of snow melting, Citizens of Earth, if you stop whatever you are doing and if you listen carefully. It may be very quiet – the dripping of water from snow-laden trees, or a slight increase in the rush of water in a small stream.

You may note these subtle changes, if your awareness is sharp, or you may be distracted by "loud noises" or "strong influences" which try – in their final death throes - to attract your attention.

If you hear these drops of water falling, or see an increase in flow, this will appear to be part of your present reality. It will be another detail added to the picture you already have. However, the picture you already have will always be reframed in every moment.

This is true always, but increasingly so at the present time which – even if it escapes your notice – is the time of THE GREAT THAW. It is up to you to decide whether these drops are "symbols" of something much greater, such as the melting of a huge glacier 1000 miles away, or the first signs of a huge blizzard.

The next question which you can ask yourselves is:

WHY CAN YOU HEAR THE SOUND OF SNOW MELTING AT THIS PARTICULAR TIME?

You can of course answer that this is BECAUSE YOUR ATTENTION IS FIXED UPON IT, but you might also reply that it is the STRONG LIGHT which causes melting and makes the effects visible.

Let us look at that statement again: IT IS STRONG LIGHT WHICH IS MAKING THE REAL SITUATION VISIBLE. The sun, in this sense, is symbolic for PURITY and PURE STRENGTH which cuts with great determination through the darkness, and which defines each shadow very clearly. This "light" comes to your earth in the form of cosmic rays which bring new information and which "upgrade" and "highlight" (there is use of that word "light" again) that which can remain strong and which stands tall, at the same time destroying that which CRUMBLES IN THE FACE OF DIVINITY because it is a force which opposes same.

Thus, you find yourselves in times of ultimate separation of dark from light. You can expect

GREAT LIGHTS,
AND ALSO ENLIGHTENED PERSONS AND SCENARIOS,
AND ALSO THE REVELATION OF GREAT EVIL
AND PERSONS WHO HARBOUR
VERY DARK THOUGHTS AND INTENTIONS.

The contrast between the two will be like heaven and hell
(and here we note that these are two realms which you on earth
have created for yourselves).

What will you do now, Citizens of Earth?

Will you simply carry on as usual?

Will you stop in your tracks, forgetting all else,
and listen for signs?

Will you assume that any signs you perceive are something which belong to a bigger scenario, a deeper pit, or a glorious new beginning?

Will you align yourselves with the "heaven" or with the "hell" which is in the process of being exposed and – ultimately – destroyed?

Or will you block everything out, numb yourselves, crawl into safe, restrictive holes and hope that everything will somehow – without any intervention on your part – sort itself out.

You have generally forgotten how important you are – that you are an integral part of that life force which strives to improve and uplift humanity.

Now is the time of the GREAT THAW – when the signs of change are all around you. It may start with a few drops of water, but it will fast become a raging torrent. Do not let yourselves be swept away or overwhelmed by this, but stand your ground, let the debris be swept away, and ask yourselves how you can contribute once the waters subside.

We are, as ever, at your sides during this sometimes dangerous and sometimes emotionally devastating period. Seraphin.

Seraphin Message 439:
THE CHANGE: BIGGER THAN YOU CAN IMAGINE
Through Rosie, 19th January 2021

Dear Citizens of Earth who are constantly quibbling about details or complaining about peccadillos or gossiping about others; what is required now is more focus on

YOURSELVES AND YOUR RELATION TO YOUR EARTH.

Imagine that your body is pocked all over with the scars of war. Imagine that you have been the object of countless Satanic experiments, which include introducing poisonous fumes and substances into your blood circulation and infesting the air you breathe. Imagine also that this air is thickened by a dense blanket of lies, atrocities, corruption and violence, and that this attacks your emotional body and burdens it on a daily basis.

THOSE WHO FEEL THIS WAY ARE IN ALIGNMENT WITH THE PRESENT FEELINGS OF YOUR EARTH, who has patiently and generously provided herself as an "experimentation ground for the rehabilitation of humans".

But what if she is now recognizing that her helpfulness is no longer useful? What would you do, Citizens of Earth, if you offer assistance to those you love but that you – for the most part – do not receive any recognition? Neither do you see any LONG-TERM IMPROVEMENT. Would you not also sigh deeply, rearrange your thoughts, change your focus and "let go"?

This may well cause a "storm", but a necessary one, just as the soul you call Jesus caused a necessary storm at the temple in Jerusalem when he turned upon the moneylenders. There is a red line which, if crossed, will inevitably cause repercussions.

The pivotal word here is CHANGE. The wind (if we can stay for a moment in the realm of weather imagery) has been blowing from the same direction for centuries, even millennia, and the weather vane has been pointing in one direction only. But weather vanes are very finely tuned and designed so that the slightest gust of wind from another quarter will immediately affect their position.

The coming storm will bring that very strong gust of wind, and it will stream continuously because it is a "DIVINE GUST OF WIND", bringing with it stability, constancy and that which is the most powerful constant, namely LOVE, which is capable of penetrating every cell.

THIS IS WHAT YOUR EARTH NEEDS. THIS IS WHAT THE GALACTIC ADMINISTRATION HAS GRANTED HER, AND THIS IS WHAT IS COMING. IF YOU, CITIZENS OF EARTH, DO NOT ALIGN YOURSELVES WITH THIS "WIND" OR WITH IT'S HIGH FREQUENCY, YOU WILL BE SWEPT AWAY.

You must face it, acknowledge it humbly and welcome it, for it is the answer to all your problems, and many will be solved immediately. However, this is a "helping hand". It does not relieve you of constant striving to learn and to improve humanity's lot. It is a "booster", if you will, to support the health of your earth and of yourselves.

This "gust" will appear very suddenly. It is pointless to deliberate when and where, squandering your energy on determining the circumstances. The weather vane will immediately point in a new direction. Our knowledge of this suddenness is what propels us today – and which has propelled us all along – is the reason why we have made so many attempts to warn and advise you. As always, this day of great change draws closer, but do not torment yourselves, trying to determine WHEN this may happen. Rather, use the time to prepare and improve YOURSELVES. Seraphin

Seraphin Message 440: WANTING THE END
Through Rosie, 27th January 2021

How many of you are presently wanting to see an end, Beloveds? How many of you are desperate to see abuse, corruption and violence disappear from the face of YOUR earth? The emphasis here is on YOUR, because YOU have an innate responsibility for what happens on this hallowed ground which – by the way – is only yours in that you are GUARDIANS of this precious space which you call your home.

To be "wanting the end" of something
means that you are in a state of want,
which indicates a very strong
LACK OF SOMETHING.

If you send out this strong energy,
SOMETHING STRONG WILL COME
TO FILL THAT VERY LARGE GAP.

and if you are in a desperate state – as many of you are – then you will not be able to wait any longer, and you will welcome that SOMETHING STRONG with open arms without fully discerning what it may do in the future.

You may be welcoming a saviour (and so you hope) but in actual fact, you may also be inviting "devilish" consequences. These can thrive because they fill one of your greatest needs, which is not "freedom" but security. With the comforting feeling that all problems are solved, you will now be able to get on with "life as usual", or whatever was usual for you.

Note here that many of you have been leading lives which you consider normal, but which actually involve the very aspects which are detrimental to your earth – a tendency to squander, waste, destroy and decry others, as well as a tendency to succumb to ego and to fail to respond to emergencies.

Wanting an end can therefore turn out to have dangerous results.

Your desperation may be so strong that your powers of assessment have no time to scrutinize the offered solution.

If one focusses exclusively on finding the end, this also narrows your view in that your whole energy is concentrated on one "point in time", as opposed to the present, and as opposed to the time AFTER THE END. What we are in fact telling you here is that THERE ARE NO ENDS, ONLY CONSTANT SPIRITUAL PROGRESSION, IF YOU CHOOSE IT, AND IF YOU WORK ON IT.

Wanting the end cements you into a position of paralysis. It means that you are "waiting" for someone or something else to take up the reins and direct what is not being directed at the moment. You expect someone else to take on full responsibility and you expect to remain inactive yourselves.

This is the sort of erroneous thinking which has led to all your problems in the first place: failure to assume responsibility, failure to correctly assess a situation, and – the most important – failure to go into action once you have realized that there are diverse powers working against prosperity, abundance, beauty and peace. They are doing all they can to promote war, division, hatred and dependence.

It is time to come into your own sovereignty, not wanting the end but making plans to propel your passage towards more positive circumstances in a continuous and determined manner, instead of sporadic weak efforts or – the worst-case scenario – no efforts at all.

Everything depends on you, not on the elites or any other "power" who have earned your trust. The future will be created in accordance with your effort and vision, and thus it is now the time to develop visions for the future, taking concrete steps towards them.

We warn you that everything will "go downhill", and that any present feelings of despair will increase.

Do not let these overwhelm you, and do not build up expectations which will only programme you to fall into another "ditch". Instead: steadily build up your skills and consider how they can be best applied to create a new era of peace.

We thank you for your attention. Seraphin

Seraphin Message 441:
UNCOVERING TRUTH, AND THE JOY TO COME
Through Rosie, 11th February 2021

The problem that you are facing, Beloved Citizens of Earth, is very much an emotional crisis, because many of you are simply going to be hit in the face by an unexpected icy blast. This is because you have not been keeping track of the "weather".

There have been many warnings or "forecasts", but you have, for the most part, not taken them seriously or have been all too ready to dismiss them as "conspiracies", and this has been so often deliberately and successfully suggested by your slave-owners.

Yes, dear Ones: the icy blast will reveal to you that you have been slaves, and that you have indeed been content to live your lives as slaves, conceding real "freedom" to your owners. As slaves you have been exploited, abused, trafficked and deceived.

There is hardly any realm of your lives – including the realms of your "entertainment"- which have not been corrupted and manipulated to serve the agenda of your jailors, keeping you "in the dark" while they continue with their perverse forms of pleasure, one of which is PREYING ON YOU.

The icy wind in your faces will bring you to a standstill and put many into a state of paralysis and shock. Some will not be able to survive this degree of trauma. They will succumb to sadness, despair and death.

Others will feel uncontrollable anger rising throughout their bodies and will resort to immediate violence. Be on the lookout for these ones, lest you get caught in the "crossfire".

Those who remain will have a very difficult situation to deal with, faced with the devastating truth of your slavery, the extreme re-actions to its discovery, and the need to pull yourselves together despite everything, and to start cleaning out the "mess". And as the "messes" are investigated and clarified, more shocking facts will be uncovered.

This will be a devastating process which only the "toughest" will survive – those who can stay the course, those who can think critically, those who can show compassion, those who can admit humbly to their own participation in the "mess", and those who can launch into creative action.

This will be your new elixir, dear friends – going into action to create new structures, a completely new system, new ways of education and self-government, new organisations and regula-tions, new opportunities and new ways of thinking.

Above all, NEW MORAL STANDARDS,

What could give greater joy, Beloveds, than righting all these hei-nous wrongs? We ask you to be strong and to look after your-selves as you move into "battle mode", so that your (self) impris-onment is a thing of the past.

You may ask: "Is Seraphin over-exaggerating here?"

As always, "time will tell" and "future proves the past". If you look well to our messages which have been provided over the last few years, you will increasingly realise their relevance to the present day, even if you were not struck with them at first reading.

We could not be more serious, and it is our pledge to help you and remind you - during the turmoil and trauma of the final days before a new start is made - that the end is glorious.

Seraphin.

Seraphin Message 442: THE NAVIGATOR
Through Rosie, 23rd February 2021

Who are you on the ship which travels through life,
Beloved Ones on earth?

How do you see yourselves?

Are you a person of importance, directing events, or are you a helpless victim, working in the galleys, or are you somewhere in between?

Do you wish to remain in the position you find yourself? Is there anything you want to change? Are you suffering or are you rejoicing? Are you inhibited or are you confident? Are you frightened easily into submission, or will you – in acute situations of discomfort – move out of the shadows and speak your truth?

Imagine you are on a ship. Are you a person of little rank, receiving orders and fulfilling them repetitively, with no room for "promotion", for individual thinking or for creativity? Do you have an official post, surveying the crew while adhering to instructions "from above", and somehow caught in the middle? Does your sympathy for the "downtrodden" override your need to "look good" in the eyes of your superiors? Or are you at the very top of the pyramid – the captain of the ship - giving orders and rarely seeing what is happening on the ship below.

There are other positions which are of importance. Perhaps you are one of those? Perhaps you are the boy who spends all his time at the top of the rigging, on look out. This will be the first person to shout DANGER.

Note that to continually be in this situation will be extremely strenuous and will give you a false view of what is actually happening. Note also that if you see ice ahead, it may well turn out to be a sea of white water lilies when you actually get there. And vice-versa. Being pushed and pulled from one extreme to the next can be extremely tiring. You will be exhausted.

The most important person in the ship are the NAVIGATORS. They will SET THE COURSE and continually check the direction and assess the weather conditions. They may be able to judge how long the journey will take, what provisions may be necessary, and what dangers may ensue.

This requires constant vigilance over all outward conditions and also all inward circumstances, including possible rebellion of the crew, or imbalance in their psychological makeup.

We are weathering a great storm presently, in one of the most acute situations which your planet has ever encountered, and if this is something you cannot see, then maybe you have been concentrating on your work "below decks". There is no possibility of "jumping ship", because this will involve certain death.

Contemplate how you fit into the global crew, and whether you are playing a valuable part in this community which is going through a very dangerous phase. Your integrity is required, your creative energy is required, your courage and compassion are required. Investigate your lives and assess whether you are in the right position, or whether there is any way in which you can improve to assist "plain sailing".

This is the topic we touch on today, because we see so many of you in a despondent frame of mind, because you are concentrating on a momentary "lull" and because you see no wind in the sails. You will not be prepared – in this mind-set – for the next ALMIGHTY GUST. Again, we try to warn you to prepare yourselves physically and mentally for the coming crisis.

Seraphin.

Seraphin Message 443:
THE MOUNTAIN OF LIES AND THE HEIGHT OF YOUR FALL
Through Rosie, March 14th, 2021

Those of you who are gradually awakening from your long slumber, your sojourn in a limited experience, your concentrated focus on one direction only, will be noticing that all is not what it seems. You will detect that something does not fit into the overall picture as generally presented, and you may start to get suspicious.

Being suspicious, critical and curious is usually – and deliberately - frowned upon, so that you return to the conviction that ALL IS WELL. If you believe that ALL IS WELL, there is no need to question or go into rebellion. Thus, you are easily manipulated.

Opinions which differ are easily crushed by specific tools which have been deliberately introduced, and here we would like to mention the whole construct of "political correctness" which keeps you neatly and voluntarily in your place. Other words, introduced purely to keep you and your thoughts in captivity, similarly dismiss any sort of criticism. It is easy to sustain a narrative and condemn everything else as a "conspiracy theory".

It is easy to immediately condemn someone who does not fit into the narrative by calling them a racist, homophobe, Nazi or anti-Semitic. These words immediately strike fear into the faint-hearted who are subsequently rooted to the spot in fear.

Such accusations are capable of stopping people in their tracks. They conjure up such atrocities, with which they are in your minds associated, that those who stand accused – perhaps for only a peccadillo – generally hang their heads and retreat into the shadows. Criticism, quite simply, is not tolerated.,

And yet, inhabitants of earth, the shadows are being penetrated. The light is now increasingly upon you, and the shadows will be no more, lending great clarity.

We are not talking here about exposure of the supposed racists and Nazis among you, who may be accused as such but who are actually presenting a critical viewpoint which will have some foundation. We are talking about exposure of those who have actually DESIGNED THESE THOUGHT PROCESSES SO THAT YOU HAVE LANDED IN A THOUGHT PRISON. THIS HAS BECOME SO SUCCESSFUL THAT YOU HAVE LEARNT TO CENSOR YOURSELVES. YOUR PRISON MASTERS HAVE DETERMINED YOUR PARAMETERS, AND YOU HAVE SUCCUMBED, SWALLOWING IT ALL "LOCK; STOCK AND BARREL".

YOU ARE SO GULLIBLE THAT YOUR CONTROLLERS DO NOT HAVE TO SET MUCH MORE INTO MOTION, BECAUSE YOU ARE TURNING AGAINST YOURSELVES.

In such a scenario, there will be less and less need for policing, because people will police themselves, turning in friends and family members with great enthusiasm, and with righteous indignation. Your slave masters congratulate themselves and laugh when they see this.

You think that we go too far with this, dear friends?

The mountain of lies is so tall that it is beyond your imagination. The mountain has a very solid base of thought constructs and erroneous beliefs which have been built in alignment with evil intent for thousands of years. Many of your religions are built on such erroneous beliefs. Humans yearn to be saved, to be led, to be told the truth, and this yearning for a saviour has been exploited again and again by people who have invented and distorted the truth, presenting it as THE REAL DEAL to hungry, dependent, needy souls, in order to consolidate THEIR OWN POWER OVER YOU.

The time rapidly approaches when you will suddenly notice a "mote" in your eye, or a distortion in your vision, or a hole in the narrative, and this will be the beginning of a very painful and harrowing journey, treading pace by pace along a difficult path up the mountain of lies, discovering your own gullibility, your vulnerability, your compliance with and ultimately your joint responsibility for despicable deeds which you would never have thought possible.

How will you deal with this, Beloveds?

We are shaken with grief when we think of the pain which you will have to bear, the desperation you will feel and your inability to forgive yourselves (and indeed, THE DIVINE always forgives, but you are cut off from divine thinking).

We have done everything in our power, through these messages and other means, to awaken you to the situation, to inform you what is going on, and to suggest how you can change your behaviour, yet this has only been taken seriously by a few who have been impelled to spread our words.

We beg you to spread this message, and indeed to spread any information which you feel is necessary to share, in face of the exposure of the mountain of lies which will inevitably come into view of all.

Again: how will you deal with this? Will you stand at the top of the mountain and simply admire the view, ignoring the fact that you are standing on a huge pile of broken dreams, broken bodies, and broken countries, to say nothing of BROKEN MINDS? Will you realise the depravity to which you have collectively sunken, and throw yourself off a cliff in desperation? These two extremes which we have just described are "the easy way out" (though in the first case, reality will hit even harder at a later stage, and in the second case, suicide is no option as you are bound to repeat the same experience, and are given the opportunity to make a more informed choice, in the next existence). The first is a stance of total denial, and the second is a stance of total capitulation.

The harder and more commendable road is to examine carefully every stone on your path – every lie – and to see where it came from, how it began to grow and who fuelled its growth. Only with a long, hard look at what you have created can the destruction of same be completed, and so that an entirely different landscape can ensue.

"What are all these lies?" you may ask.
There are many, and we will name just a few.

Your history books are censored and abominably incomplete. You have been cut off from your cosmic divine origins. You have been persuaded that you are helpless, struggling humans with a finite life, whereas you are actually eternal brings with potential beyond your belief. You have been persuaded that you need money, "entertainment", insurance and "benefits". You have been persuaded to live life in fear, rather than rejoicing in abundance. You have been told there is no cure for cancer and other serious diseases. You have been told that you are alone in the universe. You have been told that there is actually nothing beyond the world of the senses. You have been taught to fear "death", and you have been told that "death" is the end of all experience, whereas it is actually a transition to a new stage of your spiritual journey. You have been distracted in all possible ways from the spiritual path. You have been formed like clay into weak, unquestioning individuals who cannot imagine that evil exists. The revelation of pure evil in all its forms – human trafficking and consumption, abuse and murder of children, theft on all levels, experiments on humans through bio-weapons and psychological experiments, gross deception to further the agenda of those in power – these are just a few of the revelations to come, and realise also that war and genocide have also been perpetrated with your unconscious blessing.

There are very hard words, we know, but the mountain of lies is very high, and we feel it our duty, once more, to warn you of it so that you can best bear the burden of sudden shock as the truth reveals itself, and so that you can better support your astounded and heart-broken fellows.

You may ask: "Why are these revelations coming at this time?"

This is a question which requires a longer answer, but suffice to say that huge cosmic cycles are coming to a closure (yes, more is happening in "space" than you can imagine), and that you are now in an area of the universe where there is increased cosmic energy of many kinds.

These waves of energy are sweeping through your earth, causing great cleansing, where cleansing is possible, and unfortunately illness, where this is not possible. Closely associated with this "divine uplifting" of frequency, is the promise of the one you call Jesus, who knew of earth's position in these energies at this time, and who returns to survey earth's transition.

If you are in alignment with the information in this message, and if you feel that you are part of this team which is here to assist humanity though this "rite of passage", we ask you to spread our words far and wide, on every possible platform, and at every opportunity, for this will ease the process.

We stand in gratitude, Seraphin.

Seraphin Message 444: WHAT IS THE END?
Through Rosie, 27th March 2021

Dear Citizens of Earth: as we watch you manoeuvring yourselves – whether consciously or subconsciously – into a crisis of unimaginable proportions and acuteness, we shudder to think how you will react, once atrocities are exposed to all, and once you truly realise how very much you have been "had".

The deception has been complete and very long-lived, and certainly started eons before this, your present incarnation.

A number of you who do research and who are already onto the track of discovery will know that there are more things to be discovered. Others will be faced with completely unanticipated "surprises", and will thus not be able to bear this as well. This stems either from your action, or lack of action. Your discernment, or lack of discernment. Your curiosity and scrutiny, or lack thereof.

Listening to your "spark of divinity", which urges you to act with integrity, will prevent the opposite, or the deliberate ignoring thereof. And there are yet others who do not have access to an inner voice of wisdom, because they are not "hard-wired" for this.

There are some who will immediately recoil at this thought – that some are more "equipped" than others, yet this is the case. Human DNA has been manipulated for centuries, and this is something of which the majority of earth's population is completely unaware. Different "bodies" have different attributes, and it is not all fairly distributed.

You may ask why this is. Your slave masters have deliberately downgraded the masses, and upgraded the gifted or psychic few, in order to serve their own nefarious purposes.

But whatever body you find yourself in, with whatever attributes, you are experiencing all this for a specific learning purpose, and you acquiesced to this before "birth". And whatever the situation, it is your decision how to react to the present stress, and indeed to the revelations to which we refer. Many of you are feeling desperate, because you can see no END. This is a result of a very severely limited imagination and limited understanding.

At this juncture, we would like to ask you, Beloveds;
WHAT IS THE END?

Some of you, in complete despair, will contemplate suicide because they consider their lives unbearable. They cannot see beyond a brick wall, beyond a litany of tragedies, beyond a sea of sadness which will inevitably engulf them. These feelings may be overwhelming, but the people who succumb to them are those who do not recognize how they limit themselves. They "believe in" their own limited view. They think they are one hundred percent correct. They think that they can accurately predict the future, and they assess that they have no place in it, and that it will not provide them with one iota of joy. They are arrogant enough to think that they are the centre of the universe, and that they have the knowledge that this is indeed the end, and that it is better not to survive to see it. They cannot imagine that there is any other way out. They have forgotten that when they were 12, they could look back at their behaviour when they were 7, and judge that they had grown, not just physically, but on a mental level. And similarly, those who, at the age of 40 look back to the convictions, beliefs and emotional state which they held at the age of 25, will conclude that they have progressed and matured.

Such earth inhabitants are aware of their potential for growth, however difficult the present situation. They know that some new insight will occur and that a new perspective will open up, shifting their perspectives and offering new opportunities. Those who cannot do this will simply see THE END instead, and refuse to continue living.

Which category are you in, Beloveds?
Is it all too terrible to bear?

Will you have a new perspective in a year's time, even if that which you "expect" does not materialize?

Your spiritual progress – and we must say that this is the most important sort of progress - is not based of any outside event, thought outer challenges may encourage it and develop it, if challenges are met. Your spiritual progress is a DAILY AFFAIR, irrespective of the chaos which may or may not surround you, and irrespective of any ENDS you may wish for.

To fall into despair means that you have given up, that you have cut yourself off from the divine hand which attempts to guide you constantly. It means that you defy the concept of progress and that you wish to stagnate. It means that your enthusiasm is decimated, and that you allow yourself to enter a condition of paralysis and complete standstill.

If you look at the natural world, you will see that there are always cycles, in your seasons as well as in your universe. Try to place yourselves and your consciousness within these cycles and see yourselves AS PART OF THEM.

Thus you will always move with them, in full flow, leaving the past behind and moving on with ease. If you feel desperate, breathe deeply and remember this, and remember THAT THERE ARE NO ENDS. THERE ARE ONLY BEGINNINGS.

There are so many new beginnings in front of you, Beloveds, that you will be amazed, and when they occur, you will remember this very message to you, given to you in your darkest hour. Seraphin

Seraphin Message 445:
DO YOU WANT FREEDOM OR
INFLEXIBLE DIVINE AUTHORITY?
Through Rosie, 31st March 2021

Are you aware, inhabitants of Earth who are riding precariously on huge ocean waves above untold depths, that the players on your world are in turns completely ignorant, deplorably naïve, despicably evil, and anywhere in between? Do you know also that there are spies and double agents – those who appear to be evil (and who are roundly defamed as such by your corrupted press) but who are actually agents of the "light"?

Similarly, do you know that those celebrated by the media are often simply cardboard cut-outs, positioned for specific purposes as part of a specific agenda which you have never heard of, and which seeks to ruin you, degrade you, corrupt you and BREAK YOUR CONNECTION TO ALL THINGS SACRED AND DIVINE?

Do you actually ever say the words SACRED or DIVINE? Are they even part of your vocabulary? If not, the "dark side" has done its job very thoroughly, and you have failed to detect it.

Welcome to your world – the world where tolerance and freedom are touted and thrown to the masses like candies to pacify them. Simultaneously, you are bombarded with other vocabulary – slanders and condemnations which are in very regular use: Nazis, racists, homophobes, and in fact ANYTHING-PHOBES, and you use these frequently to condemn others and to foment division, falling meekly into line in accordance with your slave-drivers whose aim is to "divide and fall". There has never been such a thorough, worldwide orchestration of your minds, seeking to take control, and the majority have fallen for it, succumbing to the pressure, ensuring the so-called "freedom" of others, but thereby losing their own.

Let us be quite clear about this. You are not enjoying any freedom at all. Those who have realized this feel very oppressed by their clarity of thought, because every detail and every thin construct of falsehood is recognized instantly for what it really is – another bar of their cage. It is "soul-destroying" to live this way. This painful awakening to the narrowness of your existence, governed by your schooling, your financial system, your social, governmental, judicial, national and global systems, amounts to a "battle for your souls". Some will awake to this. Others will remain soundly asleep.

"Fighting for freedom" has become a much-used phrase. If there was complete freedom of any kind on your planet, there would be no need to "fight" for it. This very phrase indicates that there is SO MUCH standing in the way of real freedom. Also, your own concept of what real freedom is – complete freedom to do whatever you like – is also erroneous. Complete freedom, in that sense, is not freedom at all since it would encroach on the freedom of others, causing restriction, wastage, pollution of the environment, and most of all, causing IRRESPONSIBILITY.

So, what is the alternative? This is something which many earth inhabitants would completely reject, yet the end result would be similar to the results supposedly caused by your present, naïve versions of searching for freedom.

The alternative is INFLEXIBLE DIVINE AUTHORITY.

We see you balking at the words INFLEXIBLE, for your present concept of freedom suggests endless and ever-changing, fluid horizons, and we see also that the word "authority" conjures up negative pressure on you. But let us explain.

Cosmic law is indeed INFLEXIBLE. Put in very simple terms, a stone thrown into a lake will always cause ripples. This is not something you can change because you think that the water does not deserve to be disturbed, or because you think the water is suffering from being hit too hard. There is no point in standing up for the rights of water, or in standing up and condemning stones. Nothing will change CAUSE AND EFFECT.

While we are on the subject of water; water will always seek out every crevice. It is unstoppable. It cannot be caged in. It can change form – to ice or through evaporation. It will always be SOMEWHERE and it will always FLOW in the end. In a way, it is symbolic of THE DIVINE'S LOVE FOR YOU.

If we take another look at inflexible cosmic law, we will discover the inflexible law of balance. If one side of the scales is heavier than the other, it will inevitably tip. It is no use complaining that this is "not fair". This is "inflexible" in that it will happen anyway, whatever the emotions it may incur.

The biggest question is:
WILL YOU BEND TO THE AUTHORITY
OF SUCH DIVINE LAW?
WILL YOU WORK WITH IT,
OR WILL YOU CONTINUE TO IGNORE IT
AND PUT YOUR ENERGY INTO
USELESS, COSMETIC CAMPAIGNING?

WILL YOU USE YOUR ENERGY TO TIP THE SCALES
IN A POSITIVE DIRECTION?

Another example of inevitable outcomes is as follows: if a balloon is filled by too much hot air, it will burst. Your minds have been filled with so much "hot air", Beloveds (with lies, manipulated thoughts, and unseen agendas that affect you negatively), that your heads are fit to bursting. Just one more lie, one more "straw on the camel's back", and the dreaded truth will explode in your faces.

Can this be stopped, Beloveds?

NO.

BECAUSE THE UNIVERSE ALWAYS ADDRESSES GROSS IMBALANCE. THIS IS AS SURE AS A PENDULUM REACHING A POINT OF NON-MOTION – HANGING FOR A SPLIT SECOND IN MID-AIR – AND REACHING THE POINT WHERE IT MUST START ITS RETURN JOURNEY.

IT MUST SWING IN THE OTHER DIRECTION ONCE IT HAS REACHED THIS STAGE.

THIS IS AS SURE AS THE FACT THAT AN EXHALE IS INEVITABLY FOLLOWED BY AN INHALE OF BREATH.

AND YES,
THE UNIVERSE AND ALL ITS PARTS
IS BREATHING.

There are ways, of course, of delaying such outcomes – like holding one's breath for a long time, or by trying to stretch the skin of a taut balloon, or trying to freeze the water so that a thrown stone creates no ripples, BUT ALL THESE MEASURES, whether undertaken by the "dark side" or the "light side", are TICKING TIME BOMBS and do little more than temporarily postpone the DAY OF FINAL RECKONING WHERE THE BUBBLE BURSTS, WHERE EVERYTHING EXPLODES, WHERE THE FULL IMPLICATION OF ALL RIPPLES OR ACTIONS ARE SEEN AND COMPLETELY EXPOSED.

At that point, you will realise that your ideas of what "freedom" is, were completely misguided and misplaced. You will realise that pursuing "freedom", without taking on full RESPONSIBILITY FOR SELF AND OTHERS AT ALL TIMES, has actually had the opposite effect and has created a self-made prison which, in a hideous contradiction, has given you the erroneous idea that you are actually free.

What is the answer?
We have indicated this in our title:
INFLEXIBLE DIVINE AUTHORITY.

IF you recognize the laws previously described and
IF you live in awareness of them, and
IF YOUR BEHAVIOUR IS IN ALIGNMENT WITH THEM,
THEN YOU CAN TAKE UP YOUR POSITIONS
AS RESPONSIBLE CREATORS AND
CREATE PARADISE ON EARTH.

Instead of resigning yourselves to a life of limited potential and experience, you will then indeed live a life of DIVINE FREEDOM. This does not require "greatness" or "fighting determination" or "financial backing". The Divine will have your back, if you can act within the realms of Divine Law. This does not require "fighting for freedom": it requires SURRENDERING TO DIVINE LAW.

We hope that we have been able to shed light on the incredible journey awaiting you, even as you slumber and procrastinate in your small, limited corners. The world awaits you.

A clarion call is presently going out to those who have the capability to "step up" and move into this new area of knowledge, of behaviour and of spiritual growth, for the time is near when the balloon bursts. It is full to overflowing, and the explosion will not be pretty. You, with the inspiration gained from this message, will be better positioned to console, pick up the pieces and to encourage others to take up the exciting journey ahead.

When all this happens, you will remember this message and go back to it for guidance and solace. It will help you to move forward. Seraphin.

Seraphin Message 446:
THE POINT OF A NEEDLE, AND PINPOINTING
Through Rosie, April 22nd 2021

Dear Citizens of Earth
who find yourselves in a very critical period.

The basic problem is that some of you KNOW that the situation is critical (and you respond to the call that something of great import and great radicality must be implemented to reverse negative trends), while others just "find themselves" in the thick of unpleasant circumstances.

Rather than using critical thinking to assess WHY this arose in the first place, they go either into quiet retreat, denying it all, or they fall into loud complaining mode, naively repeating thoughts and information

WHICH HAVE BEEN DELIBERATELY PLANTED INTO PLANE-TARY CONSCIOUSNESS IN ORDER TO PRODUCE STRIFE, TO FOMENT CONFUSION THROUGH DISINFORMATION SPIKED WITH TRUTH, AND ULTIMATELY TO CONTROL.

Yet the more this control is now exerted, the more people will awake to it, and this is one way (of several ways presently being implemented) in which your noose is being loosened.

What is your perspective on this, Beloveds?

Are you awakening?

Are you prepared to dedicate yourselves to a global cause, righting the fate of your earth and your fellow inhabitants, or are you complacent, tolerant and resigned, allowing everything to "carry on as usual"?

IT IS TIME TO IMAGINE!

Can you imagine your great creative power?

Can you imagine the plethora of inhabited planets
in the entire Creation?

Can you imagine what the inhabitants of other planets might be
thinking as they observe you at this very precarious moment in
your history?

Can you imagine that your personal behaviour will
"make or break" history?

Can you imagine the vast wealth of wisdom to which you have
access, if only you will "go within" and ask?

Can you imagine the microcosm which sits on the
point of a needle?

Can you imagine that this microcosm,
in all its intricacies and tiny parts,
is a reflection of the macrocosm,
of the entire "multiverse"?

Do you think in such dimensions?

Do you realise the glory of eternal learning?

Do you know the deep satisfaction of serving to uplift others,
or are you so stuck in your ways that you are defeated by the
pockets of negativity which are constantly being thrown at you by
your media and by your governments?

Do you choose to "think big"?

Do you choose to remain cowering in your holes?

EVEN MORE SO THAN ANY OTHER
PERIOD IN YOUR HISTORY,
YOUR PRESENT CHOICES MATTER.

THE MORE PRECARIOUS THE SITUATION,
THE MORE CRITICAL YOUR ACTIONS,
AND THE MORE INFLUENCE
YOU EXERT THROUGH THEM,
FOR BETTER OR FOR WORSE.

You are the deciders, the way showers, the courageous heralds of a new era. You will receive help and protection, if your intentions are good, however difficult the situation may be. We will not see our beloved ground crew helpers peter out on their last breath, burdened to the ground by oppression.

Remember that we are here to support you and uplift you, for this is our elixir in an experiment which is unprecedented. And because it is unprecedented – including unprecedented levels of hidden evil and long-standing control mechanisms – it is so difficult for some of you to fathom.

Some of you are simply flailing around with your arms, feeling utterly helpless, as if no one will do anything or come to your rescue.

YOU MUST TURN INTO THE RESCUERS!

You must sharpen your reasoning.

You must examine all aspects minutely, and find the holes.

YOU MUST PINPOINT THE FAILING MORAL FIBRE which is destroying the very fabric of society, and you must PICK UP THE NEEDLE and repair those very patches, step by step and stich by stich.

Does this sound like a long and momentous project, Beloveds? IT IS! It is part of EMERGENCY OPERATION EARTH who has been suffering for millennia from your heinous behaviour. You can hardly imagine that it will go unnoticed. She is affected by your every, breath, word, thought and action.

We have made many calls in the past, and this is another one, as the plots thickens, and as ABSURDITY RAISES ITS UGLY HEAD ON A DAILY BASIS.

To those who see all this, and who are desperate, know that all this is temporary and that it will end, and know also that the QUALITY OF YOUR BEHAVIOUR – IN EVERY SMALL AND LARGE THING – BRINGS YOU CLOSER TO CLOSURE AND TO THE FINAL STAGE OF AWAKENING.

Following this, only the humble, the curious, the morally worthy and the proven servants will remain. Thus, we send out this, yet another "last call".

Some of you may shake your heads cynically at this, and laugh knowingly, saying that there have been so many "last calls" and warnings about things which have not (in your eyes at least) materialized. To you we say; you arrogantly assume that you know all, but you do not. You assume that decisions have been made (and then "deserted"), WHEN YOU ARE ACTUALLY STILL IN THE PROCESS OF INFLUENCING THE DECISIONS. You assume, actually, that you are IMPOTENT, and we would ask you humbly to reverse this way of thinking.

VALUE YOURSELVES as important pieces in this "chess game", and know also that the game will finish with "checkmate" before a new game can begin. Our gratitude goes to those who take our words to heart. Seraphin.

Seraphin Message 447:
THE MANY FACES OF PERFECTION
Through Rosie, 30th April 2021

Dear Inhabitants on earth who wallow in the slime and dirt of your own making. Are you waking up to this yet?

In this critical period of Spring 2021, you could be said to be neck deep in the mud, and astonishingly, not everyone has noticed it, because they are so used to seeing IMPERFECTION all around. They are used to struggling. They are used to stagnating and not being able to move freely, whether this is physically or mentally (and we would also remind you that there is a strong relation between the two).

To be mentally blocked (and thus to underscore the lack of flow in the sense of no new ideas or forward thinking aimed at problem solving) means that this blockage must manifest simultaneously on a physical level, in the stiffness of your limbs, as well as the stiffness of your lives, and in a general inability to change.

This change, however, is desperately necessary. As we have already said, you are up to your necks in mud, and your bodies are buried beneath water soaked sand on a beach where the TIDE IS COMING IN RAPIDLY. It is only a case of whether you realise this – whether you hear the noise of the waves, or whether you turn your head towards the noise. The flow of the tide is inevitable, as is the ebb of the tide, and you will be forced to notice it, even if it is at the very last moment.

WOULD THIS NOT BE THE PERFECT MOMENT, BELOVEDS, TO DO THIS VERY THING? TO TURN YOUR HEADS THE OTHER WAY, TO OPEN YOUR EYES AND TO CORRECTLY ASSESS THAT YOU ARE IN GREAT DANGER?

Wouldn't there be PERFECTION in that moment, and in that great realization, and wouldn't it be the PERFECT opportunity to scream for help, or indeed to warn the others who are still looking in the opposite direction, distracted by something completely different, in danger of losing their lives?

And would not all events leading up to this precarious scenario, which is now a case of life or death, be PERFECT in the sense that without them, THIS DEVELOPMENT IN THE MINDS OF THE POPULACE WHO ARE BURIED UNDER THE MUD would never have taken place?

And would this not also be the PERFECT LEARNING LESSON for all observers of this scene who have meticulously noted how the layers of mud have thickened over eons of time, and how the minds of your planet's inhabitants have simultaneously degraded, all culminating in this one massive bulldozing of old paradigms and offering you a new chance to start again?

Could there be anything more PERFECT than this to provide onlookers with intricate knowledge of how to prevent such catastrophes in the future? Are you already getting a new idea about what PERFECT really means?

Thus, THE PATH TO PERFECTION may seem to be the exact opposite of perfection, yet it is an essential tool to achieve perfection. Perfection is a goal, yes, but perfection can also be experienced ON THE WAY, so we could say that PERFECTION IS THE WAY. Another way of saying it is that PERFECTION ALREADY IS. This is a very difficult pill to swallow for those who consider themselves victims in dreadful circumstances. It may take many years, and considerable hindsight and self-reflection, to see certain awful situations as "stepping stones" to a new awareness, and new mode of behaviour, and a new outlook on life. But we would like to make this completely clear:

YOU ARE NOW, AT THIS VERY MOMENT, IN A VERY, VERY DIFFICULT PLACE, EVEN IF YOU DO NOT NOTICE IT, AND DESPITE THE TRAUMA YOU WILL FACE, IT IS THE KEY TO TRANSFORMATION.

It is like being in a prison, and not knowing it until you walk out of the door. Rejoice that these "dark times" will finally be resolved, and that the LIGHT will reign, in all areas of life, supporting everything which is in alignment with the Divine. It is this – being in alignment with the Divine – that you will have to learn, Beloveds on Earth. For many, it is your final chance.

Slowly, you may be realizing that PERFECTION IS ACTUALLY A GAP WHICH PROVIDES AN OPPORTUNITY
TO ACT IN A MORE PERFECT WAY.

If you look around you, you will always find someone who you think is "more perfect" than yourself. This is programming yourself into continuous discontent. This is programming you to follow others rather than focus on personal development.

If you progress spiritually every day, in some small way, this is the PERFECT WAY TO GO. You can only judge yourself by your own yardstick, not by someone else's yardstick. Otherwise, you will never achieve independence and complete sovereignty.

To go even further, you will never become
SONS AND DAUGHTERS OF THE DIVINE
(or GOD, as you love to say),
manifesting the very best you can.

Do you think we are asking you to reach too far? On the contrary, these are only the very preliminary steps on the amazing journey in front of you, if you are determined to proceed along this path of PERFECTING YOURSELF.

If we move from a personal level to something wider, such as the field of technology, then we can ask ourselves the question WHAT IS PERFECT TECHNOLOGY? It may seem to be that which is quicker, faster and more economical. However, if such technology is applied FOR NEFARIOUS MEANS, then it is no longer "perfect", but aiding and abetting crime.

Again, we would like to show you here HOW IMPORTANT YOUR COLLECTIVE MIND-SET IS, AND HOW IT BEARS INFLUENCE ON YOUR REALITY. The future huge leaps in potential which technology will bring in the areas of health and curing "incurable" diseases, is beyond your present imagination, but it is up to YOU whether this materializes, or whether such technology is to be exclusively applied in war scenarios to pinpoint certain parameters, objects or conditions, in order to destroy or mutilate them.

PERFECTION IS CONTINUOUS EFFORT

Even if a project has been completed to perfection, or if a house has been renovated to perfection, then it only "lasts" for a certain period. If our awareness lessens, or if our attention roves, or if we are distracted, or if we are corrupted, then the perfection will slowly – over time – start to crumble.

The people who are involved in a project are always changing. Their initial enthusiasm and dedication may wane due to other pressures, due to sudden tragedies, due to new alliances or the desire to move away, or the desire to start a family.

Staff may function perfectly for a while, but when a new person arrives on the scene, every member of the group has to readjust before all feel comfortable and at ease again, especially if the new individual has strong opinions or new ideas, or lags behind on their duties.

In personal relationships with friends, family or colleagues, there is a danger that "outside forces" – the "economy" or "demand" or "debt" for example – will add new ingredients to the mix, just as outward forces – nature, weather, animals or insects – can undermine the "perfect" renovation of a house.

Thus constant PERFECT MAINTENANCE AND ADJUSTING AND REASSESSMENT is required in all areas.

AFTER PERFECTION

And so, after all this has been "taken to heart", what happens next? Changing conditions as well as a change of location will always bring new challenges and learning lessons. The journey is always upward and never-ending.

We would advise you, in these turbulent times, to keep your minds PERFECTLY ATTUNED TO THE DIVINE ADVISOR WITHIN YOU, as well as PERFECTLY READY TO GO INTO ACTION AS A RESULT OF THEIR ADVICE.

The "action" on your world will culminate at the PERFECT TIME, and will – whether you like it or not – it will result in the PERFECT NEXT STEP FOR THE EVOLVEMENT OF EARTH'S POPULATION.

We leave you with this, yet another warning:

Your views and your lives are about to be shattered, but that it will be glorious once you have picked up the pieces, working together in PERFECT CO-OPERATION.

Seraphin

Seraphin Message 448: BLESSINGS IN DISGUISE

Through Rosie, 15th May 2021

Beloved Citizens of Earth: the benefit of pain is that it will force you into action in order to end an abominable situation. If you are still slumbering in soporific mode, cosy and comfortable in your self-constructed illusions, then you have not reached this stage, but we do warn you that those comfortable bubbles will burst, resulting in agony for the great majority.

Even you will be surprised and "taken aback".

Why would we (and many other "helpers" guiding you through this mess towards an era of "light and life") expend so much energy over so many years, using various methods and various scribes as our voice, in order to try and reach you? It is because we are intensely aware of this very great agony with which you will be faced, and the very great feeling of betrayal and hopelessness with which you will have to deal.

This sudden and painful awakening may be so unbearable that some of you sleepy ones will fall dead on the spot, as if you have suffered a very sudden and severe heart attack.

We are very sad to have to say these words. Our compassion for your situation – in fact for all global inhabitants – has impelled us again and again to prepare you, in order that this "blow" may be lessened.

Those who have already gone through various stages of pain, who have done their investigations thoroughly and who have developed authentic behaviour due to dedicated work on themselves and on all hindrances preventing true communication, and who have learnt to commune with the "Divine", will not be so surprised, and will not be subjected to such a serious degree of shock.

You ones can be grateful for your "dispensation period" of slow but methodical learning over many years, as hard as it may have been, and as tortuous it is to know about continuing corruption and atrocity, with no definite end in sight.

When you see the sudden shock and desperation of others, and the consequences thereof and the resulting trauma, you will fall upon your knees in gratitude, recognizing the comparatively gentle nature of your awakening, during which you were allowed to proceed at your own pace of learning.

This will seem to be a BLESSING IN DISGUISE.

This period has also allowed the "waiters" and "seekers"
to "enjoy" a period of comparative quiet.

This may seem like an incredible or absurd statement today, as you observe developments on your planet,

YET THE PACE OF CHANGE AND
THE PACE OF ACTION REQUIRED FROM YOU
WILL INCREASE EXPONENTIALLY IN THE FUTURE,
TAKING YOUR BREATH AWAY.

If you have not already developed methods of centring yourself, of quickly settling priorities, of courageously stepping out in public, or of executing decisions in alignment with Divine guidance and in accordance with Cosmic Law, then you will have great difficulties in adjusting and in playing the roles originally assigned to you.

This is a "hiatus" for you to prepare yourselves along the lines we have just mentioned, to develop your skills and to prepare your materials, and to keep up with your contacts. Most of all, it is time to develop your visions for a better world. For example, if you want to build a TEMPLE OF THE DIVINE SELF (a favourite project of this scribe), then use the time to design it. If you have valuable information or wisdom which you want to share, or projects which will benefit others, PUT THEM TO PAPER.

Do not waste your time, Beloveds, but anticipate how you can be the most excellent agent of development and positive change. You are brimming with potential, Beloveds, and it is your decision HOW TO TRANSLATE THIS INTO ACTION for the benefit of those who will remain to rebuild this world. Seraphin.

Seraphin Message 449:
RECOGNISING THE GREAT UNSEEN
Through Rosie, 24th May 2021

It is part of the cosmic law of balance that where there is one side or "weight", there is also the opposite, and to reside at the fulcrum is the perfect balance. If there is below, there is also above. If there is a macrocosm, there is also a microcosm. Where there is light, there is also dark (allowing the light to burn all the more brightly, by the way). Where there is outside – the material, physical world, there is also inside – the world of thoughts, motivation, feelings and intuition – The world WITHIN which each human uses to manifest the WITHOUT.

By the same token, that which is SEEN co-exists with ALL THAT IS UNSEEN which, if you consider the small wedge of "reality" you are experiencing at a certain time in a certain limited space (consider in your musings the myriad numbers of inhabited planets in the universe) is actually a huge chunk of the unknown.

It is time for you, inhabitants of earth, to stop proclaiming your high levels of knowledge, your "cutting edge" research, your overviews of your situation, your "intellectuality", your supposed expertise in your narrow fields of experience, and succumb to the more than obvious fact THAT THERE IS SO MUCH YOU DO NOT KNOW, and that your portion of knowledge is incredibly miniscule in comparison with the vastness of space, and what happens there.

We do not wish to crush your sense of self-worth with this sentence; we merely wish you to observe and understand that your views and understandings are necessarily limited and that there is SO MUCH THAT YOU HAVE NOT SEEN.

Hence this message, encouraging you to open your eyes to all sorts of new explanations for old stories, new angles on accepted "proof", new solutions to old mysteries, and new encounters with beings and concepts which, in your limited understanding so far, you might consider "supernatural" or "impossible".

We would ask you to consider the word "surprise". In the course of your lives, you will encounter many surprises. These encounters or experiences would not be surprises at all if you were familiar with all possibilities, all potentials, all variations, all available countermeasures, all dimensions and all different perspectives. You may say that it is impossible to have such an overview, or to see with such eyes, yet – and this is another aspect of THE GREAT UNSEEN – there are "great beings", which we would like to describe as "celestial", who are capable of this, and much more, and who understand EVERYTHING WHICH IS NOW ROLLING OUT ON YOUR EARTH PLANE.

If you asked them "What is really going on?", they would be able to respond immediately and succinctly, IF this information is something which you, in your mental and spiritual capacity – are able to digest and use appropriately. Yet if you are not "ready" for such information, it will not be provided, because it would harm or SURPRISE or SHOCK you so much that you would stop dead in your tracks. This would mean that your chance of moving forward has been taken away from you, and no such great beings would wish to be the cause of such stagnation or lack of forward movement, since it is exactly this which they wish to promote. If you ask them, they will say that it is their intent to raise you – by your own efforts but with their guidance – to their own level of comparative omniscience and wisdom. The soul you refer to as Jesus is one of these, who said "YOU CAN DO AS I DID, AND MUCH MORE".

How can it be possible that you overlook the existence of such great souls, whether on or off planet? Because your minds are closed, refusing to accept this possibility. Your minds are limited, trained to focus only on the SEEN – that which is material and physical.

To focus on the "seen" will allow you to live from day to day, often in a comfortable way, but your life will be lacking thrust, the desire to serve, the fulfilment of excellently executing a worthy project, the joy of communing with nature, the ecstasy of discovering a hitherto unknown truth, the exhilaration of knowing that you are in alignment with the Divine, or the bliss of holy co-creation.

Your unseen guides will push you at tremendous pace should you acquiesce and concentrate on spiritual development and service towards humanity. And this "humanity" is also only that which you can SEE. If your devotion here on earth is obvious, is sustained, is recognized as being of value, you will surely be encouraged and promoted to help UNSEEN WORLDS in the future, after having experienced this "less-than-perfect" situation on this earth, in combination with your efforts to remedy same.

Would you say that it is wise to confine yourselves to physical perceptions? To rely on your eyesight, as far as the eye can see, but no further, on your sense of touch, or on your ears alone? You only need to look at nature to conclude that there are creatures with more superior senses than your own (the eyes of eagles, or the ability of birds to hear a worm underground, or the capability of bats who know how to sense each other in the dark).

Are there any other non-physical feelings on which you rely? Some are familiar with the "gut feeling" which prevents them from doing something which they feel is wrong. Others may feel strong feelings of intuition (and here we would like you to understand that this is DIVINE INTUITION, FED TO YOU BY YOUR OWN PERSONAL UNSEEN GUIDES). This is an UNSEEN REALM which, if you wish to progress, must assume a major part of your mental landscape, which you should practice accessing so that your trust in these pieces of advice increase with every experience, so that it becomes COMPLETELY UNSHAKEABLE. This can be practiced to such a degree that you are constantly connected with your inner advisor, which is a fragment of the Divine, or with your advisory angels, in the sense that your decisions are guided by them in every moment. This is not continual subservience: this is surrender to excellent guidance in order to achieve glory.

Your thoughts, emotions, plans and actions, whether seen or already manifested on the physical plane, are all fed into earth's genetic mind – another UNSEEN REALM. Some might refer to this as the "morphogenetic field" or the "united field of consciousness". You always contribute, whether you realise it or not, whatever the quality of your input. And the input will create a "body of work and instructions" which is available to others.

If you remain purely on the physical plane, thinking that your actions and thoughts have no consequence whatsoever, you are sadly wrong.

KNOWING THIS, HOWEVER, WILL IMBUE YOU WITH A GREAT SENSE OF POWER, FOR YOU WILL KNOW THAT YOUR ACTIONS ARE HAVING AN INFLUENCE ON OTHERS WHO ACCESS THE GENETIC MIND FOR INFORMATION.

This is so different, is it not, inhabitants of earth, from the narrative you are fed by your media, by your "leaders" and by your religions, who insist that you are small pawns in a big chess game, and that pawns must sometimes be sacrificed for the GREATER WHOLE.

WE SAY "NO". PAWNS ARE NOT ALWAYS PAWNS. THEY CAN DEVELOP INTO SAGES, EXPERTS, HIGHLY SPIRITUAL SOULS IN THEIR OWN RIGHT. THEY CAN BECOME KINGS AND QUEENS; GODS AND GODDESSES.

We know you will cringe at this use of the word GOD, but this is because you have been trained to think that GOD is an all-powerful, strict and somehow forbidding entity who regularly metes out punishment, rather than an OMNIPRESENT POSITIVE CREATIVE FORCE RESIDING WITHIN US.

THE GREAT UNSEEN PAST

Another aspect which is presently still unseen is the UNSEEN PAST. You have swallowed the offered version of the history of your world "hook, line and sinker". Indeed, you are all like fish who have swallowed the bait, and who cannot take the time or who have not the capacity to consider that there may be alternative narratives. You have been grossly deceived.

When you learn of the true history of your planet and all the negative lineages which have been controlling its development (or lack of development, since it is their aim to keep the power and money for themselves), then you will hang your heads in shame. For some, it will be unbearable, as we have previously mentioned. Others will be consumed by remorse and guilt. Here we would say that self-forgiveness will play a great role for those who can muster it, and who have the ability to "restart" their own history, like taking up the pen to script a completely new story on a blank piece of paper. We use these forceful images to show you that there is so much that you do not know. Your horizons will inevitably expand, and this is part of the process of "enlightenment" and of progressing on a spiritual plane, which will inevitably be the cause of positive developments on a physical plane.

THE GREAT NUMBERS OF UNSEEN ENTITIES

Apart from the personal guides and unseen helpers present on your earth to help you progress, the "multi-universe" is populated with trillions of beings who are more advanced than yourselves. Again, we are not referencing physicality here, but rather their state of mind, which is purely benevolent. As a consequence, these are entities of much higher vibration, and it is this which may cause their bodies (the vehicles they use for expression and experience) to become "lighter" and larger. We relate this to again show that it is the STATE OF MIND WHICH CREATES PHYSICAL REALITY.

Hanging onto your particular world – because it is of low vibration (the consequence of wars, violence, corruption, pollution and all other manners of abuse) – are many low-vibration unseen entities who have "died" but who have not yet managed to move on to the next stage of their existence. Their sorry influence – sometimes designated by you as "possession" - is a warning to you on the earth plane of the consequences of "falling low" and the consequences of getting stuck in destructive thought patterns or mode of behaviour. Stagnation means that the learning process has stopped. Those souls who "haunt" the living are those who cannot "let go" and move on, and this is mirrored in those they afflict, who are a mirror of their plight, not being able to "let go" of addictions or of low-level living, rejecting all aspiration to better things.

THE GREAT UNSEEN OF SUBLIME SUGGESTION

One great unseen of which many are largely unaware is the level of propaganda which is levelled at you specifically on a daily basis, whether this is the news you hear, the confusion which is deliberately instigated, the words of the music you listen to or the "entertainment" you are offered. We will concentrate on "entertainment" for this is exactly what is offered to help you "relax", and which fills your mental landscapes to such a degree that you cannot turn off your phones or televisions and spend time SIMPLY THINKING, which would lead to much insight and which would allow you to shut out all distractions and noises, allowing you to hear the VOICE OF THE DIVINE WITHIN.

Much comes under the name of "entertainment", and while this is – in your assumption – supposed to help you wind down, it is actually doing the opposite. Pulsating rhythms, loud noise, packed emotions, voyeur situations and "cool" music and performances in the name of "art" do not make you relax or provide food for the soul. They fragment, burden, and depress. Even if you feel superficially energized, this takes its toll on a subconscious and UNSEEN level.

This scribe has just watched a number of "modern dance" choreographies which have been highly celebrated by the (controlling) media. The movements are startling, unusual and interesting, but at the same time they are jerky, robotic, broken, fawning and lascivious. This is movement which is not actually movement. The holy flow is broken, and if you align yourselves with this, praising the ingenuity or novel aspects of such a performance, YOU ARE SIMULTANEOUSLY DENYING THE LIFE FLOW IN YOURSELVES. The same is true for music which may be soothing to the ear, like jazz, a genre which many of you love, but which SPLITS THE DIVINE WHOLE INTO FRAGMENTED PARTS AND DOES NOT RAISE YOU TO THE HEIGHTS REACHED BY LISTENING TO A DIVINELY INSPIRED AND HARMONIOUS COMPOSITION.

To conclude: after reading and digesting all this you might say HOW SMALL, INSIGNIFICANT, POWERLESS AND UNSEEN AM I, yet that would show that you have not fully understood what we are trying to point out here. The GREAT UNSEEN should not intimidate you, but inspire you to greater heights. It opens up a huge vista of possibilities, allowing you "to bravely go where no-one has gone before". For you are all unique, capable of impacting the experiences of others in a positive way, and this should be your focus WHEN THE GREAT UNSEEN IS REVEALED TO YOU, AS IT IS PROGRAMMED TO DO.

This revelation is part of the "end times", the end of huge cycles which promote GREAT CLARIFICATION ON ALL LEVELS. Thus, you can expect GREAT SURPRISES, which may at first appear to take the form of calamities or tragedies, but which ultimately lead to GREAT PERSPECTIVES FOR A WONDERFUL FUTURE WHICH WERE PREVIOUSLY UNSEEN.

With these thoughts we leave you, Seraphin.

Seraphin Message 450: THE DIVINE INDWELLING
Through Rosie, 27th May 2021

What does it mean, Beloveds, to be "divinely indwelt"?

Does it mean that an over-powering force will suddenly invade you without your will?

Does it mean that it will reside in every cell, irrespective of the defence you put up? Does it mean that you will recognize it in advance and put up your hands and say NO, NOT HERE, NOT NOW, I'M NOT READY?

What does being "divinely indwelt" mean to you,
inhabitants of earth?

Are you even acquainted with the word "divine", or what it actually means, as far as your behaviour is concerned, or as far as your mission is concerned, or as far as other people are concerned?

You may wish to ponder these questions, as they will prepare you for what is coming. You will be receiving an invitation, and it is up to you whether to accept it or not. Of course, if you are already busy, or occupied, or if you have got something else planned, then – you know how it is with invitations – you will immediately say that you have not got the time, or the capacity, and you will reject it outright.

If you are only partially committed to your "normal" activities and your "normal" train of thought, then you may entertain the thought of an invitation, but if you are in a state of constant flow and flux, reflecting on every step, living in the moment, you may indeed be ready to accept any invitation which is forthcoming, especially if it resounds in the timbres of your inner being, especially if it reminds you of something glorious from the past, especially if it exhilarates you to the point of no return.

These are your options, inhabitants of earth: to choose between your sorry, dull, stuttering path on the way to a dimly defined goal, or to join with the divine light which is coming, so that you can co-create with it to form a completely new, enlightening, joyous and exhilarating path. It is your choice.

We hereby give notice of the arrival of such an invitation, and we invite you to consider the consequences in advance, for those who choose the path of darkness and refuse the light must move to a place of darkness and cannot remain on a planet which is destined to be flooded with this same light.

Again, we beseech you to ponder your choices carefully, and to awake to the possibility of your lives changing around completely on this beloved jewel of a planet, or whether you prefer to keep staring in one direction, plodding along the same old beaten path which never changes. Seraphin.

SERAPHIN'S QUESTION AND ANSWER SESSION

These questions were posed by spiritual seekers residing all over the world, seeking advice on specific issues in a public internet forum. These answers from Seraphin were received telepathically by Rosie Jackson between 2015 and 2017.

Seraphin's Initial Address

Dear Friends on Earth. For your great attention in matters of great importance, I thank you. This scribe has penned and collected my teachings for a considerable period, and while they travel the internet, they are still pieces which may come across as impersonal, or sometimes even harsh.

You live in harsh times, Beloveds, and therefore strong words are often necessary to counter what is going on both IN PLAIN SIGHT and BEHIND CLOSED DOORS. And some of these CLOSED DOORS are indeed YOUR OWN CLOSED DOORS, dear ones.

My invitation here is for you to ask questions and OPEN THE DOORS THAT YOU ARE AFRAID OF OPENING, which you know will change your lives forever, if you do.

It would be my joy to accompany you on those first faltering steps as you leave your old views and convictions and harmful situations behind, in order to move into a plain with vast horizons.

Seraphin

QUESTION ON OUTER APPEARANCES

Seraphin: people nowadays attach so much importance to their exterior, for example the decoration of their homes or their cars. It is very important to them that everything is perfect and they take their pride and self-esteem from that. And anyone who does not live up to their standards is criticized and excluded. There is so much energy spoiled in this way, which in my opinion would be much better spent in taking care of their children, pets or gardens – the living things. Would you please comment on this?

ANSWER FROM SERAPHIN

Greetings to you. Indeed, you have pinpointed here one of the main diseases of your global society - to focus on cosmetic exterior beauty rather than the inner beauty which radiates kindness, care, generosity and respect, and which conceives of itself being in service to others.

While beautiful areas and housing and gardens can be very soothing to the soul, the soul who lives in such surroundings but who continues to be selfish, unloving, violent and abusive, WILL PERPETUATE THE GIRTH OF NEGATIVITY WHICH IS SMOTHERING THE PLANET.

Regarding standards; high standards in cleanliness and functionality are to be praised, and they can also serve as inspiration for others, yet those others must be MADE TO SEE FOR THEMSELVES that this might be beneficial. If orders appear from on high, in the form of criticism, they will not be able to accept this.

It is your own experience of and promotion of high quality relationships, goods, standards and the resulting happiness, which will be the key for others to pursue similar standards.

Regarding standards of behaviour: the general "standard" on earth is very low. We advise reflecting on the qualities of the soul you call Jesus to see what you can aspire to.

QUESTION ON PARENT / CHILD RELATIONSHIPS

Dear Seraphin, I am very concerned about my son who is not successful in his studies, but doesn't want to try anything new. He also eats too much. What can I do to help? What can he do?

ANSWER FROM SERAPHIN

Greetings to you, devout mother, yet you also need to let go somewhat. Your concern for your son is extremely worthy, as supporting a child is one of the most demanding and rewarding and important tasks which this earth experience has to offer.

You strain to give your children what you consider to be "a good start" in life. Yet there will come a point when the energy for the "start" or the further continuance of existence and for the creation of one's future trail must be transferred to the child itself, and this moment should be accompanied by a feeling of intense elation on the part of the child - that finally, they can themselves choose exactly what they wish to do.

If this moment is overwhelmed by accompanying fear, then the momentum is lost. And momentum will actually come to a standstill if both parent and child fail to notice that this moment of independence as opposed to interdependence has arrived. To attempt that transition at a later stage involves emotional pain and difficulties all round, including a keen sense of loss and even of betrayal on both sides.

This is where a very well-developed degree of sensitivity should come into play on the part of the parents, involving questions like HOW MUCH CAN I LET GO and TO WHAT DEGREE SHOULD MY CHILD NOW BE SELF-RELIANT?

To retreat, as opposed to offering further help, is sometimes more loving than to continue along familiar paths. To increase this sort of awareness – of where both people stand as individuals – is very necessary in this situation you describe, as well as frequent (but not incessant) communication to check and recheck positions.

If there is a feeling of being abandoned by the child, increased eating may be a result. If continuously and generously supported, the child will subconsciously know that there is not actually much need to go into strenuous action. If assistance and suggestions are always made to the child, then its creativity does not get a chance to develop. If there is an overt show of extreme concern, self-confidence will suffer, with the result that the child may become convinced that it cannot "recover" alone.

All these elements have an influence on the child/parent relationship which ideally should develop into a relationship between responsible adults who care for each other deeply. We hope that this may have shed some light on the possible causes. Of paramount importance is also that you, as a role model and as inspiration, act in the sort of way which you would wish him to behave. We wish you much strength and also joy, Seraphin.

QUESTION ABOUT HELPING A RELATIVE

Dear Seraphin, I am very concerned about a close relative who has become suicidal after the breakup of a long engagement. She sees no future for herself and insists on torturing herself emotionally by hoping for some kind of reconciliation. We have given her all the best advice but she refuses all help. What should we do in such a situation?

ANSWER FROM SERAPHIN

Greetings to you who is so concerned for the welfare of this relative, and who has administered so many plans and who has tried so many ways of reaching her in order to provide a new and positive perspective, to little avail.

This lack of success has very little to do with the quality of your teachings. We feel it very necessary to say this - that this lack of understanding or appreciation is not a reflection of you. It is as if you are separated by a high, black wall, and it does not matter how many times you try to break it down, and it does not matter how large the goodness in your heart or how overflowing your intentions, if there is no crack to admit these to the other side. The wall is over her own making, and thus her responsibility. This may sound cold, yet we know of your deep compassion, and this will certainly not stop for this member of your family, whatever her choices and however she reacts. This is the very best you can do for her: be consistent, be positive, be joyful that you yourself have received insights in meditation or through signs which have helped you through similar sad periods, and attempt to BE that which you wish her to be.

QUESTION ABOUT PROVIDING FINANCIAL HELP

Dear Seraphin. If a person is struggling financially, is it appropriate to send help? If so, does that help or hinder the path of that person's journey, if surmounting financial issues are part of their challenge in this lifetime?

ANSWER FROM SERAPHIN

Greetings to you. With respect to offers of financial help: the construct "money" is unfortunately an issue which soils many relationships, moving them often into the realm of self-interest rather than into the realm of authenticity and genuine mutual affection. If you consider for a moment how all relationships would be affected if money suddenly disappeared or became useless overnight, then it will be clear to you what basis your relationship rests upon. Many foundations are shaky in that DEPENDENCY is often a strong but deceptive glue which cements them together. It is in fact DEPENDENCY which you would wish to avoid if gifting someone, whether this takes the form of financial help or otherwise. To remove someone from their RESPONSIBILITY through financial aid is to make them dependent on you, and it does not encourage them to seek alternatives.

It is wonderful to be compassionate and to offer help, yet if this degenerates into continuous assistance when there are actually other possibilities, including changes in behaviour on the part of the receiver which would turn around their situation of LACK, it is better to desist and allow them to GROW through their self-made dilemma.

QUESTION ABOUT THE ELDERLY

Dear Seraphin, I have a question about the elderly – the percentage of the elderly in my country is growing because we have fewer children. Youngsters are at school or at university, and adults are working – usually far from their parent's homes. After retirement, the elderly often live alone with little money and nothing meaningful to do. So they become ill, and this at least gives them an opportunity to go see the doctors where they meet other patients in the waiting room. This certainly is not the life meant for us. How will this change? Are there some jobs for which the elderly are particularly qualified?

ANSWER FROM SERAPHIN

Greetings to you and thank you for your concern about the elderly. Yes indeed: many live very solitary and lonely lives and do not take much part in social interaction. Any such interaction is purposely organised rather than spontaneous. If you look at the way your society works - OR ACTUALLY THE WAY IT DOES NOT WORK - and if you collectively really understood how low quality your lives are in the sense of true contact and support, you would try and change something immediately.

Concerning illness, this can be the joint result of many factors, including physical stress and mental stress combined, including a degeneration in physical material of the body and of food, and including the LACK OF LOVE. Growing ill to gain attention is a strategy developed by individuals when they are small children. If it worked for them then, they may subconsciously also know it might work for them later also. We would ask you all to visualise the ideal situation for those who are getting on in years and who no longer have much physical strength. Imagine yourselves as such, and how you might like to live. This is the situation now.

Following the changes, there will be improvements of many kinds, including the quality of food, air, medical treatment and community spirit. "Life expectancy" will rise. All - irrespective of age - will be encouraged to consider HOW THEY CAN CONTRIBUTE TO SOCIETY. There will be no people "out of work" or "retired" in the sort of structures you presently uphold. Money, also, will become a non-issue.

There are no particular jobs for which "elderly" across the board are particularly qualified. There are many very active elderly people at the moment who follow their interests and who are also of service, despite frailty or "age". It would be interesting for those who are weak and who feel weak to investigate WHY THIS SHOULD BE SO, and HOW ANOTHER PERSON OF THE SAME AGE CAN BE SO DIFFERENT.

Know that your own behaviour and decisions HAVE GOT YOU ALL TO THE POINT WHERE YOU ARE AT PRESENT. In this we return to the topic of RESPONSIBILITY FOR THE LIFE YOU HAVE CREATED. If you see someone who appears to have a particular hard life or hard "fate", please consider that you know very little about the background or the mental or spiritual state of this person, to say nothing about the "karma" which they have chosen to work off in this incarnation. Your compassion is commendable, but you are necessarily ignorant of the truth of their situation.

Regarding the "percentage" of the elderly growing fast: a great many souls will choose to leave this earth plane and start anew, either on other planets or in new incarnations, so the ratio of "old" to "young" will change anyway, according to those choices. Also, the fear that there are too many old people for young people to support (based on tax paying and the paying out of retirement money) will no longer be an issue due to less emphasis on finances. After a time on "galactic welfare", your attitudes towards all this will change considerably. Also, the fear that earth cannot nurture so many people is justified. The global population will be regulated so that this does not happen again.

QUESTION ABOUT ELDERS

Dear Seraphin: a common cultural practice in older traditions is to respect elders (inherently for the wisdom they provide). This of course has lost its inherent value in current modern culture for many reasons. In times to come when we are rebuilding a new society, what function will these elders perform? I notice that as a grandfather, I have a great impact on my grandchildren and can further their inner growth.

ANSWER FROM SERAPHIN

Greetings to you, and thank you for offering your services to those little ones seeking their way through a quagmire of information and disinformation. You may be sure that they will gravitate towards those who can offer them an alternative and who can convey wisdom rather than indoctrination.

Although their "knowledge" in the traditional sense is not yet grown, their inner knowing is so much more advanced than many still on this earth plane who are their superior in YEARS ONLY. Yet this is not a competition; the path of each individual is just that: INDIVIDUAL. And all those you encounter will have an effect, whether positive or negative. For those children presently growing up in your society filled with propaganda of all varieties which CORRUPT INDIVIDUAL THINKING and which DEBASE THE MIND AND BODY, children would presently do well to look to persons they can trust in the older generation in order to regain their balance and open their perspectives.

But not all children have access to such "elders". What we are looking forward to in the future are communities where EVERYONE IS RECOGNISED. The words of wisdom may come from the older generation, and they may come out of the mouth of "babes" also. The focus is not the origin of the thoughts but the QUALITY. Age, in this sense, will become less relevant and will also become less of a separating factor. There will be no expressions of OH, SHE IS JUST A CHILD AND DOES NOT KNOW BETTER. And there will be no expressions of I AM SURPRISED THAT HE WANTS TO SPEND A WEEK WITH AN OLD LADY LIKE ME. All these inhibitions and preconceptions and judgements of oneself and others will fall away with time.

As we have said before many times, the focus is on the individual LEARNING JOURNEY. If this involves seeking advice from others, this is fine, yet each person individually - whether young or "old", must make their own decision as to whether the advice given is appropriate or useful. It will become normal for a soul with less experience to instinctively seek out souls with more experience, and age has nothing to do with this.

The celestials have a wealth of experience at their fingertips and can also assess very quickly which piece of information of advice will further your growth the best. This is, among other things, why they will be excellent counsellors for you. We realise that these words will cause problems for those who consider themselves "old and wise" and who use their supposed experiences as a means of wielding respect. This is an ego-based attitude and it prevents them from approaching others with a truly fresh mind as they are rooted in the past and in their wonderful previous exploits. This prevents true communication and true understanding of another. It is time to look at these attitudes very seriously and to humbly seek another way.

QUESTION ABOUT DEALING WITH GRIEF

Dear Seraphin: my question is one concerning intense grief and disappointment, especially regarding the present-day conditions on earth, knowing how those came to be, and knowing what Gaia is going through because of them. I have tried to combat these feelings, but sometimes they are overwhelming. Is it possible to completely release these energies? And is there something that may be blocking me from doing so?

ANSWER FROM SERAPHIN

Greetings to you. Know that you will soon SPREAD YOUR WINGS and move forward in a way not thought possible so far. Not small but GREAT THINGS lie in your path; GREAT THINGS achieved and GREAT ISSUES to solve. We entreat you connect often with your GOD WITHIN who is always encouraging, always comforting and always capable of providing DIVINE WISDOM when you feel you are caught in a "rut". The "rut" you speak of is indeed a very large one, equivalent to the very deep injury sustained to earth. Yet, if the thought of this paralyses you, if you concentrate on this or cannot think about other aspects, then the dark side are rejoicing because they have managed to make you INACTIVE. This means INACTIVE IN YOUR SERVICE TO THE LIGHT SIDE. To pour out a never-ending flow of reports on atrocities and pollution and abuse and murder IS AN IMPORTANT PART OF THEIR STRATEGY. If you focus on this mostly, you will of course land in deep depression from which it is difficult to surface.

Therefore, know of these things but BALANCE them with things of the light, by which we mean time in nature, with good friends, in silence with yourself in meditative pauses, with uplifting music and with anything else which occurs to you. We need all the support we can get to see this phase through, so we entreat you to be optimistic and to FEED THAT OPTIMISM YOURSELF by the methods already described. To take on the burdens of another - in this case of your earth Gaia - is to LOSE PART OF YOURSELF if you allow this to overcome you completely. This means that you cannot serve in the capacity planned. This means also that you take away responsibility from the other person involved.

Gaia, your earth, is now at a point where her decision and her self-preservation mechanism is kicking into position. She requires support on the ground rather than those who are so sad that they cannot react. You may ask within what blockages there may be preventing you from regarding other as "victims" and from being overly affected by what you consider to be their "fate" and by how they have been WRONGED. It will be beneficial for you to regard everyone - including YOURSELF - as a creator of your own story. This is valid for Gaia also. As you will see in the times to come, she also will take matters "into her own hands", while still under celestial surveillance, and with galactic help. This should be your favoured stance also.

QUESTION ABOUT DIFFICULT RELATIONSHIPS

Dear Seraphin: right now, I am in a very difficult relationship with my wife. We have very nasty fights. She has a lot of low-vibration feelings - anger, intolerance, jealousy, rage, revenge, depression. I have talked to her, but she doesn't listen. She does not share my view of spirituality. I think she may still have a chance to change, but I don't want to interfere in her journey either.

ANSWER FROM SERAPHIN

Greetings to you. This is the result of INTENSE CHOICES. This we say due to YOUR choices here on earth, including your choice of spouse. To think that you are "interfering", therefore, in her life-stream and experiences is erroneous. She also chose you. As in all relationships, you have chosen to learn from each other and are to some degree a reflection of each other. When clashes are extremely serious it is necessary to try and "step out" of the situation and see it from a very distant and objective perspective, almost as if you are a stranger being confronted with this for the very first time. How would you behave towards her if you were a polite visitor, only in the household for a short period? Perhaps this is an exercise which you can try out.

Moving from your "lower self", which has difficulty dealing with anger and tantrums and whatever other excesses are thrown at you, into your "higher", polite, understanding visitor-self (to continue our previous image and suggestion) may well have the effect of relieving the intensity of this situation. Instead of being unbearable for you, it may then become more of a situation of interest which you are observing.

If you embark on this, then this is a form of assistance for her, and it also lightens your load. It may well also increase her respect for you. This may seem like roleplaying - like being someone who you are not - but in this case, we would ask you to throw away any fixed notions or ideas you have about yourself/your identity and to try and discover that part of yourself which is absolutely centred, which is absolutely authentic, which is firm and unswayed and which can regard the situation from a distance without coming to immediate conclusions or judgements.

Remember that everything is open. All can be changed in a moment if attitudes change. If you make such a "move" in this relationship-system, the other half - your wife - must necessarily make a "move" or change too. She will start to react differently.

QUESTION ABOUT NURTURING NEW SOULS

Dear Seraphin. There seems to be a common feeling of being a "stranger in a strange land" that I witness in myself and others that tend to think deeply about their life.

Within the incoming group of souls of the current generation (often called indigo) this seems more common than uncommon.

What are some of the recommended guidelines in helping these incoming souls adjust to life?

Do they need more of a protective atmosphere or open atmosphere around them in their early years?

ANSWER FROM SERAPHIN

Greetings to you, friend to be. All strangers are friends to be.

It is your great challenge on this earth to inhabit a physical body which may not - in the vague stirrings of the deepest recesses of your memory - be a familiar vehicle of expression for you.

Yet here you are, with the specific intent of experiencing these momentous times, in a body so that you can actually participate on a physical level.

When you enter a new room or a new area of study or a new group of people or - in this case - a new world - you will always feel strange at first.

Yet with time this will dissipate. This trains your skills at adapting and making creative use of your possibilities, even if they are - in your perception - limited.

We would ask you to try and focus more upon the opportunities - especially in this unprecedented situation - rather than on what is lacking or what could have been, as this line of thinking can lead to downward spirals that seek pity from other observers and which push you - irrespective of how slight this may be - into the role of victim. To flourish in your role as active entrepreneur in full flow is your aim.

Regarding incoming young souls: many already intrinsically possess a level of deep wisdom which they are rediscovering / "remembering" as they grow up. What such souls need is reassurance of their Divinity and support in the sense that they are recognised for their special talents and qualities. These should be nurtured as best as possible by those who understand them.

QUESTION ABOUT PARTNERS AND FAMILY

Dear Seraphin, like many around me, I am divorced and I wonder what went wrong. So, I would like you to answer the question of how to find the right soul-mate. Do you have some good advice about how to live in a good partnership in harmony and joy? I am thinking also of all these scattered and broken families in our world. Many parents do not see their children regularly, let alone their grandchildren, if there are any. This causes so much sadness and loneliness. Is the old concept of family wrong? Do we have to adopt new ideas about what family means or are the traditional concepts worth keeping? And in this context, do children need to be in contact with the elder ones, to see their good example? When I grew up it was so much easier for me to take advice from my grandmother than from my parents. My children did not get the benefit of this sort of relationship. Is this one reason why the relations between family-members are so loose nowadays?

ANSWER FROM SERAPHIN

I thank you, who are much loved by us, for this very worthy question. It is indeed essential to understand exactly what forces are having a detrimental effect on relationships and families in order to construct supportive, prosperous and stable communities in the future. One of the biggest realisations to come to terms with is that there have been many forces attempting - through propaganda and enforcing their own detrimental and selfish agendas over a long period of time - to insert VERY LARGE WEDGES OF SEPARATION between all manner of people and nations, and this includes the sexes and different generations.

Mutual respect and equality, in a continuous state of helping each other and searching out each opportunity to do so, with the only goal of uplifting the other to their highest potential, is what you should be aiming for in relationships of whatever kind. This is much more than a sexual exchange. This is joining as one in the sense of combining in a joint energy stream. And in accordance with the saying WHAT YOU GIVE, YOU WILL RECEIVE, this attitude will benefit yourself as well.

Children are a treasure. Couples who wish to embark upon the journey of looking after such treasures, surveying their upbringing so that it is wholesome, protected and informed about all principles as laid out in the LAWS OF CREATION, will in future have to state their intentions very seriously and will also have to undergo training in preparation. Whereas this "job" of bringing up children is presently largely left to those who do not have close personal ties to the children themselves, this will become more and more the sphere of the parents themselves. It is something which should not be "delegated".

At the present, much delegation is undertaken in the name of having to earn money, in the name of having to relieve stress, in the name of others having better qualifications to teach, yet it is the parents who know the child best, and to whom the child has the most trust, especially in the early years. To recognise parents as worthy teachers is something which must be developed.

This may, in the final analysis, be seen as the most important task which there is. This is a very different perspective from the role of "housewives" in your present society, where women are made to feel unworthy, inadequate and inferior. The high number of divorces results in part from the failure to recognise the seriousness of the task of raising children, in part from the financial issues which arise from this, in part from the lack of respect between the sexes (a negative energy which has been perpetrated over many, many centuries), and partly due to the insistence on "rights" such as the "rights" of the so-called feminist movement, which has caused many separation processes.

The independence of woman from their enslaved state has been very important, however it has backfired in some ways, causing ego issues, and resulting in separation rather than resulting in a balance in which both halves are equal. This is a very broad subject, so this has just covered a few aspects. If we are to take the matter further, I would note that close family units should ideally be many and strong, but that in the end everyone should be regarded as family, and as all members of the global family. In such a world, nobody can ever feel alone, lonely or unsupported. This is the vision you will be moving towards. Hold it in your hearts as we move through the next stage of this journey.

SERAPHIN ANSWERS QUESTIONS ON BEHAVIOUR

QUESTION ON THE REASONS FOR ABUSIVE BEHAVIOUR

Dear Seraphin, could you please tell us something about homicide and other abuse to human beings? Is this happening due to an "unknown reason" (from "past lives" for example), or is it only a manifestation of our unconsciousness and lack of love? Is there any "difference" between the people who kill somebody without any remorse, and those who regret it and kill themselves afterwards?

ANSWER FROM SERAPHIN

Greetings again to you. You show courage in the posing of your questions. Taking the life of another - cutting of their present life stream and thus preventing the soul concerned from choosing the time of its own departure - is against the laws of balance. It means that you have cut off that person's free will, including the termination of plans still to manifest. While there may be other influences from previous traumatic events, whether in this life or seeping through as memories of past lives, this is still a

CONSCIOUS DECISION IN THE NOW, and as such,
ANYONE COMMITTING THIS CRIME
IS WHOLLY RESPONSIBLE FOR IT.

Showing deep remorse for such an act will have a positive effect, yet how can that remorse be shown and lived if the next act is simply to take one's own life? This is also against the laws of creation and does nothing to alleviate the pain one has caused. It is simply an attempt to escape facing what one has done. This is a cowardly answer to the issue. And escape is actually not possible, for if you take your own life, then you will be strongly advised to "repeat" problematic issues in your subsequent incarnation in order to find a better solution. Those who kill without remorse are sowing the seeds of being treated without remorse. It is high time for the hearts on earth to soften, to sensitise yourselves to your self-created carnage, to put away your knives and guns, and to sew love so that you reap love. For this is actually - in the very final analysis - what everyone is looking for, and what all grave disappointments are based on - the lack of constant unconditional love. Give this and you will receive it. Do not discuss whether this sort of homicide is better or worse than that kind of homicide, rather MAKE THAT DISCUSSION REDUNDANT.

QUESTION ON FORGIVENESS

Seraphin: although I have learned much about forgiveness, I am still having a bit of a problem forgiving a couple of people that I feel did terrible things to my family. I try to see it as part of my experience and theirs, and that we were all here to learn from each other. I am still working on that, but I'd like to know if I have achieved that hurdle.

ANSWER FROM SERAPHIN

Greetings to you. We salute you for raising your hands to the stars in trust when surrounded by situations which anyone else might regard as unusually "depressing". We commend you for that strength. This is the image we see of you, overriding difficult situations and coming out of them with deep wisdom, ready to face anything new which comes your way. You will know when you have achieved that hurdle of which you speak, because if you have, you will not have to ask this question any more. You will then be "over the hurdle" so to speak, and it will no longer concern you, but we see that you are still partly involved with this.

We advise daily practice of the "figure of eight" visualisation process, whereby you are seated in one half of a figure of 8, while the person you are having an issue with sits in the other half. Imagine yourselves in this position, talk to each other, but do not cross over into the "space" of the other. In this way, without having to face these people on a physical level, you can learn to "endure" their presence (without wishing them gone or without wishing that you had never met) and you can also learn to talk to their higher selves with a regard to finding out their motives in this situation. Thus will you better understand, and thus will you better be able to release this episode in your lives.

QUESTION ABOUT ADDICTION

Dear Seraphin: I have a question about addiction, because I grew up with addicts. I observe many people around me even today that are chained by various dependencies. Will addictions be extinct on the new earth?

ANSWER FROM SERAPHIN

Greetings to you and thank you for your question. I rejoice indeed in this opportunity to convey my thoughts to you on the various issues which occur to you. Your experience with the addiction of those around you has served in a big way to strengthen your own path. Do not underestimate the power of this - to come through this as an observer of those who are not resting at all in their own sovereignty.

They have lost their connection to their sovereignty due to a number of reasons. This may involve laziness, this may involve deliberate self-sabotage, this may involve a feeling that they are victimised or cut off from others (I would add here: cut off from the DIVINE). When it becomes clear to them that the world as they perceive it is very different from reality, they will be forced to reflect very deeply on their behaviour and they will be assisted if they truly wish to be free of their addictions. This is, as with all issues, a personal choice, and this choice will be made very clear to them. It is, in fact, a fantastic learning opportunity which will greatly enhance their feeling of DIVINE SELF, should they embark on that adventure.

Those who are not capable of making such a decision will follow a different path, but you can be assured that all will receive the chance to implement positive change. The new earth and its peoples will have to conform to the following framework:

TAKING ONLY WHAT ONE NEEDS.

So taking more of one substance, thus leaving less for others, will not be permitted. For those who stay on earth, the following will be very clear:

SELF INJURY IS NOT BENEFICIAL
TO THEMSELVES NOR TO SOCIETY.

The human "material", i.e. the physical body of humans on this earth is in dire necessity of upgrading, and as this will be uppermost in the consciousness of the remaining people, they will strive to live in a healthy and health-enhancing way.

QUESTION ABOUT SURMOUNTING LONELINESS
AND FINDING ONE'S MISSION

Dear Seraphin. After all the upcoming changes, will this feeling of seclusion and loneliness finally be gone from our planet? And until then, how can we work within ourselves to get rid of it on an individual level?

Additionally, would it be right to assume that our mission in this life - and in any life really - is actually improving ourselves? And would this not reflect on every aspect of our lives and thus on the lives of others and on the world itself?

ANSWER FROM SERAPHIN

Greetings to you, whose present perception is growing, and whose eagerness to progress shows clearly in the way the question is phrased. Your comments of the feeling of loneliness which many people experience is very poignant. This is so widespread, yet the basic fact that YOU ARE ALL BROTHERS AND SISTERS OF ONE UNIQUE AND DIVINE GLOBAL FAMILY has not entered the consciousness of the multitudes.

The ruling emotion on your planet is – at the moment – FEAR. This is almost immediately activated whenever you perceive something or someone as being very DIFFERENT FROM YOURSELF. This has caused incredible divides in all sections of your societies, and it has been a tool for exacerbating all manner of conflicts and wars, whether national or individual. Even the family unit has been under attack in this way so that family members – despite the intensity of their joint experiences – are estranged from one another instead of providing mutual support.

How is this fear to be eradicated?
It cannot be erased by simply saying STOP BEING AFRAID.

We would ask everyone to look at their lives and their present position in it and look back along the long row of incidents which brought you to this point. Along the way, you will recognise all sorts of "coincidences" and chance encounters or seemingly miraculous offers of help or signs which have propelled you in a certain direction. For others, whose position is far from that they would wish to experience, I would ask them to similarly look back and discover the occasions where advice or signs were given, and which you then proceeded to ignore.

IF YOU CAN DISCOVER SUCH PATTERNS IN YOUR PREVIOUS LIFE WHICH HAVE PUSHED YOU INTO THE RIGHT DIRECTION, KNOW THAT THIS WILL CONTINUE AND THAT YOUR GUIDES AND PERSONAL ANGELS ARE ALWAYS ATTEMPTING TO DRAW YOUR ATTENTION TO SOMETHING WHICH WILL INITIATE YOU INTO THE NEXT STEP AND OPEN UP THE NEXT PERSPECTIVE ON THIS, YOUR SPIRITUAL LEARNING JOURNEY.

WHEN YOU HAVE DEVELOPED THE TRUST THAT THIS IS REALLY SO, **THERE IS NO ROOM FOR FEAR**.

THERE IS ONLY COMPLETE TRUST THAT
ALL WILL WORK OUT FOR THE BEST.

At this juncture you may ask WHAT IS THE BEST?

This is part of the questions that you have posed. The best is:

SELF-IMPROVEMENT AND DISCOVERING ONE'S OWN TALENTS AND POTENTIAL, IN ORDER TO SERVE OTHERS AND IN ORDER TO MAKE THIS WORLD A "BETTER PLACE".

In this you are completely accurate in your surmise, that working on oneself is of extreme importance, and that this is continually a WORK IN PROGRESS.

We would like to add that THOSE WHO KNOW THEIR EXACT MISSION HAVE ALREADY LIMITED THEMSELVES. You can set the course, but the achievements are still out of view, and the achievement – if work and discipline and attention is lavished generously, will bring you to levels of action and understanding OF WHICH YOU COULD NOT PREVIOUSLY CONCEIVE. We thank you for your important question on spiritual progress. This applies to all souls globally. With respect and love, Seraphin

QUESTION ABOUT HUMANS KILLING EACH OTHER

Seraphin: why does man kill?

ANSWER FROM SERAPHIN

Why indeed, dear friend, do humans kill? This is a temporary phenomenon in the spiritual journey which must be overcome if the journey is to continue. To kill is ending the present life-stream of a living being before it is time for them to move on. It is also PRETENDING TO BE GOD, as only the DIVINE AND THE CELESTIAL REPRESENTATIVES of such, in combination with the DIVINE PART OF SELF, is allowed to initiate this very final stage. Killing is, so to speak, stepping very seriously out of line, cutting off THAT WHICH IS SACRED and UPSETTING THE BALANCE. This world of great IMBALANCE has been brought into this situation mainly through mass killings and also the MASS KILLING OF THE DIVINE SELF in the sense that human is cut off from the godly self – indeed the knowledge of this has been systematically thwarted – and remains mostly in contact with the low, bestial self which gives in to base instincts and fear. To move up and above this is a blessed act – a huge landmark in the progress of human, and many should have SUCCEEDED and many more WILL HAVE THEIR EYES OPENED TO THE FACT THAT THEY HAVE BEEN SERVING DARK FORCES WHICH HAVE INSINUATED OPENLY AND SECRETLY THAT KILLING IS KOSHER. The use of this word brings me to a certain practice of killing common to those who are known as "Jews". Some believe it is ordained that animals should be killed in a certain way. Others believe that it is "better", for example, to kill a chicken while it is sleeping.

THERE ARE NO HUMANE WAYS TO KILL, BELOVEDS.
THIS IS YOUR GREAT MISTAKE: TO THINK THAT THERE ARE RIGHT AND WRONG WAYS OF DOING SOMETHING WHICH IS GOING AGAINST THE LAWS OF CREATION ANYWAY, TO THINK THAT THERE ARE DEGREES OF PURITY, TO THINK THAT IT IS ALRIGHT TO KILL (i.e. EAT AN ANIMAL) ONLY ONCE IN A WHILE, TO THINK THAT THERE ARE "GOOD" WAYS TO HARM OTHERS.

You have "reframed" your thinking to the extent that it is fully deformed, to the extent that that which is beautiful is considered vile, to the extent that that which is vile is pronounced sacred. This is a corruption of your MORAL SYSTEM, PUT INTO PLACE BY THOSE WHO OPPOSE THE HEAVENLY ORDER. Yes, it is shocking to see people and animals killed, yet you partake in it. You may say that you do not understand it. You may feel helpless. But as all acts, there is a reason, which is the slow but steady corruption of your moral impulses over many ages. You have taken part collectively in this process of degeneration and it is time to reverse same.

QUESTION ABOUT HUMAN FAILINGS

Seraphin: what is the line we have to cross, if we want to leave our human failings behind? I wish to serve in my best capacity.

ANSWER FROM SERAPHIN

Greetings to you. With respect to the area of "human failing", we would rather refer to it as "human progress". To fail, in the minds of many, is a very negatively nuanced word. It is used often in connection with failing to pass a test or an examination. Consider the situation on more spiritually advanced planets: while examinations can be set in the pursuit of finding excellence, and in the pursuit of finding optimal candidates for certain areas of service, they do not at the same time "condemn" those who "do not get the grade" to other areas in which they are not interested, or which they consider more demeaning than the one attempted. Each is placed according to their ability and each is respected for that contribution. All wish to increase the quality of their service and use all opportunities to do so. The challenge is to change your world from one which divides people into winners and losers into a population which is steadily searching and putting energy into their desired avenue of service. This is not a race course with cut off times or those who fail to make the finishing line or who collapse in a heap en route:

IT IS A CONTINUOUS JOURNEY WHERE EVERYONE MOVES AT THE PACE OF THE SLOWEST. We mean this in the sense that the "slowest", or the one whose PROGRESS is moving forward BUT AT NOT SUCH A GREAT SPEED, is as much part of the community as those spearheading its progress. That there may be "mistakes" on the way due to lack of information is more of a problem on your world as opposed to these other planets:

here, there is deliberate attempt to misrepresent and to HIDE PERTINENT INFORMATION. Yet still, the searching mind on whatever level can be sharpened to peel the layers of dirt away. This is not dependent on intellect, but often on plain common sense and on taking some time to COMPARE and REMEMBER instead of simply saying THERE MUST BE SOME EXPLANA-TION FOR THIS, and leave it at that. This is called intellectual laziness. It is not possible to make a "mistake" knowing better. If you know better, to continue doing something which you KNOW to be wrong is a deliberate negative action for which the negative consequences will be reaped by the individual perpetrating them.

What is "lack of information"? With the gift of your internet, so much information (and disinformation) can be accessed. To sort that out, your effort and discernment is required. In addition (and indeed as a very important complement to this) you also have the option of "going within" to receive the intuitive answer through your connection to the DIVINE LIBRARY OF KNOWLEDGE which is installed for this planet.

Concerning your intention to serve in the best possible capacity, we applaud your intention. More you cannot do than intend this and to react to whatever is presented to you. While you may be familiar with your present surroundings and the people surround-ing you, you cannot estimate how they will react under duress and under the sudden revelation of new information which will rock their world. We advise you to do your best, as you are doing, and to let go of any worries or worrying scenarios which are oc-cupying (and perhaps also obstructing) your thoughts.

Know that your guides are and will always be present in order to help you - whether you are aware of them or not - when the mo-ment comes. To worry is to start reacting in fearful ways

BEFORE ANYTHING HAS HAPPENED, and this in turn could trigger the "worried" reactions of others. Like attracts like. So move forward in full confidence, and infect those around you with that confidence.

QUESTION ABOUT SUICIDE

Seraphin: we know it's against cosmic law, the Law of Life, to take the life of another, least of all one's own, so I want to ask: What happens to an adult when they cross over after committing suicide and prematurely ends their incarnation? What are the procedures for dealing with these ones, as well as those who commit suicide after shooting their whole family? Are these cases what they appear to be, or is there, in some cases, an agreement between a single soul or a group of souls (a family for instance) to end the incarnation after a certain purpose or task was achieved? Are suicides thus always "bad" or may they some-times serve another less obvious purpose?

ANSWER FROM SERAPHIN

My greetings to you, and thank you for PUSHING FORWARD. I address you thus because you are demonstrating the DESIRE TO KNOW which will bring you far. If everyone really dedicated some time to this, they would always have burning questions to ask. Yet if they are so encumbered by everyday duties and dis-tractions, there will be "no time" to enjoy such contemplation. But it is indeed THE RIGHT TIME to start with this, because if the questions are not addressed, they will keep burning, and will eventually burn down the structures - on a mental level - which you have conveniently constructed for yourselves. This will result in TABULA RASA, which is a very destructive and radical way of achieving clarity and overview, yet not the easiest to undergo. It involves shock and loss. Thus, we encourage you to make enquiries BEFORE this happens.

Your world will be plunged into shock. The more you prepare yourselves, and also the more able you are to let go, the easier will be your passage, and the larger will your capacity be to help others who are stranded or straggling.

And now to your question. In general, ending a life-stream - whether this belongs to another or oneself - is AGAINST LIFE. You can see the results of being AGAINST LIFE in many phenomena in your world. The destructive streak runs through so many areas of your experience. The whole idea is to TURN THIS AROUND so that you become exhilarated, joyous and creative beings. To be creative and to create your own story is your main purpose, in alignment with the laws of creation which - as indicated by their very name - assist in this creative process.

The nature of your question indicates how low you - as a collective global nation - have sunk as regards your positive, energetic, creative possibilities. To even consider destruction would be - for other communities on more highly spiritually developed spheres - a complete impossibility. Why is it, oh children of earth, that you allow yourselves to be pulled to the path of destruction? The contemplation of suicide is the culmination of this way of thinking - the very lowest level - in that it signifies not just the end of your experience here, at a point in time which is not foreseen - but that YOU ARE DELIBERATELY CUTTING OFF YOUR OWN CREATIVE ENERGY WHICH ALWAYS HAS GREAT POTENTIAL. Who has taught you, dear children, to despair? Who has taught you that there is sometimes no way out?

The font of your spiritual inner source is great and inexhaustible. There you can always find the answers, but from this you have been cut off by succumbing to propaganda, deliberately placed disinformation and by your decision to focus on the physical and material.

Suicide, therefore, is a symptom of a wholesale REJECTION OF SPIRITUAL FORCES. Those who commit suicide are rejecting their innermost sacred selves and their innermost potential to deal with the situation. However dreadful it may appear to them, there is an answer accessible from within, if sought.

To drag others down with oneself, disregarding their own potential and cutting off their energy stream, is likewise reprehensible. Such souls are taken into "care", as it were, and are made to see the seriousness of their actions and the disastrous consequences. They are urged to correct that as soon as possible.

The only way in which suicides are "not bad" is in that they indeed serve to "wake up" those around them, spurring them on to try and understand something which, initially, completely defies understanding. This involves much distress, but it starts a huge internal search which - in its own very special and individual way - will help that individual face certain aspects of their behaviour which they would have preferred to keep undercover.

It may also inspire them to help others who have undergone a similar process and who are struggling with the consequences of someone committing suicide. Your respect for life, including your own, should be paramount, Beloveds. This is indeed a sorry chapter in the history of your planet, in that the lack of spiritual teaching has permitted such occurrences to increase.

QUESTION ABOUT THE SUBCONSCIOUS MIND

Hello dear Seraphin. My question relates to the nature of the subconscious mind. As far as I can tell, the subconscious acts as a sort of storehouse for information, emotions and experiences we undergo, filing away this information, emotion and experience so that we can retrieve it when it believes it will be useful to us. The subconscious doesn't seem to judge the "right and wrong" of what happens, but simply programs itself to put behaviours on "autopilot". Sometimes these contribute to our wellbeing, but often subconscious programs are harmful to us, misaligned with our higher self's intentions and are ego-driven. Yet the reason these programs are in place are because the subconscious is ultimately seeking to secure a positive underlying intention (such as the person who is looking for comfort and love through smoking cigarettes). I'm also curious if you can address if the above statement is accurate and tell me what exactly occurs in the layers of human consciousness when unsupportive subconscious beliefs are at play. That is to say, is the subconscious mind is, at its core, a collection of beliefs (thoughts that have been thought repeatedly), which lead to emotions which then lead to actions OR is it the subconscious primarily emotions which lead to thoughts, which lead to actions, or neither?

Also, if there exists a negative core belief such as "I'm unworthy", how does the subconscious energetically "send the message" through the consciousness of the individual to be processed and acted upon?

 Does this occur in the emotional, mental and physical bodies all at once? Is it somehow mediated by the ego and/or higher self or any other aspect of self?

Am I correct in assuming that when such an unhealthy core belief and its accompanying emotions are exposed to the higher self-consciousness), they will disappear/integrate whereas when they are "filtered" through the ego, they just expand as a means of calling the individual to greater consciousness and alignment with the soul? Lastly, is it the subconscious which suppresses negative emotion or the ego, or both? And is all of the suppressed emotion we carry ultimately the result of lost aspects of consciousness from previous experiences that are energetically trapped within and calling out for integration by the higher self? I apologize for my litany of questions, but it's a challenge to keep this condensed and I'm passionate to understand this subject better.

ANSWER FROM SERAPHIN

I greet you and extend my deep thanks for your thoughtful and detailed analysis of (and thoughts about) the subconscious mind. It may be beneficial to others to consider that the "subconscious" is an area of intrinsic knowledge which is present but not out in the open in the sense of being obvious and easily accessible. What we call subconscious knowledge is hidden.

The commonly held thought is that this is held in the mind, yet the body also holds the memory of everything we have experienced and everything we have thought, and all emotions we have been through, whether they have been expressed or not. The most interesting aspect of this is those emotions / feelings which have NOT been expressed, since these are the hidden ones, and the ones which can sometimes emerge at inappropriate times in extreme situations, when they are not so appropriate, thus causing shock or even violence to those surrounding us.

The "subconscious" can also be compared to a computer running on automatic in the sense that it (and our bodies) store all information in certain places. Some of these "files" are always accessible. They are "open" all the time. They run like a programme. Our very first choices in childhood are the components of this programme. If, when we are hungry, we decide to scream immediately and come to the conclusion that no food is forthcoming if it does not arrive within the next two minutes, then a programme of disappointment or a programme of *"I am not worthy"* can be formed. If one is hungry and decides to start crying after 5 minutes, the programme running may be *"Let's wait and see. I think it will work out in the end"*. And the baby which knows intuitively that his needs will be met will not cry at all, thus running a programme of *"I have everything I need"*. Thus is CONFIDENCE or FEAR birthed at a potentially very early stage. These are just a couple of example of core sentences which may be running your own particular programme.

The key to tracking these programmes down is to OBSERVE ONE'S OWN REACTIONS, ESPECIALLY OBSERVING ONE'S OVERREACTIONS, AT ALL TIMES, especially when dealing with strangers, for so many of you will push the blame for conflicts onto another person you think you know well. If the same conflicts appear with strangers, then this will force you to realise that YOU are a major factor in the equation.

Another method of bringing out the cellular memory of the "subconscious" storage is to carry out certain physically exhausting exercises which push you to the limit and develop self-awareness. These can quickly produce extreme situations in which that which has been hidden in the "subconscious" for so long, is forced to emerge, in order to be looked at. The more one involves oneself in these methods, the more observant and objective one becomes. The challenge is to look at oneself and one's behaviour and to say "OH, HOW INTERESTING! IS THAT HOW I REACT?" rather than to launch into conflict and into who is right and who is wrong.

So yes, dear seeker: there is a storehouse of information, emotions and experiences. In this, as in all processes, pieces of it will emerge at a time which is appropriate for the learning process. It is not possible for you to be overwhelmed by that which is TOO MUCH. If you are familiar with this principle, you will not feel crushed by developments. Instead you will feel a rush of adrenalin as you realise that yes, you are capable of dealing with this because this is exactly the right time for it, as devised by your DIVINE GUIDANCE.

I must reiterate that it is your own awareness of your thinking processes, instead of simply succumbing to what one think one needs, which requires development. It is easy to reach for substitutes for love, but if you think about this clearly, it will be obvious that no love is being gained through this. If one persists with this or any other self-afflicting and SELF-UNLOVING habit, it will be even clearer, as your sphere of activities and your focus and probably your circle of acquaintances will be reduced as a result.

Bringing such realisations out into the open requires conscious effort and it is recommended that the concept of oneself as a divine being with a divine connection be integrated into the consciousness of such a person. Thus will alternatives be provided, the best alternative being LOVING ONESELF AND OTHERS, AS THIS LOVE WILL BE RETURNED TO ONESELF. Those who ask for help will receive, even if the form that the help takes may appear to be unattractive and "wrong".

This is a huge experiment, Beloveds, into which you can enter with GREAT ENTHUSIASM, or which you can drop from one minute to the next. It is your choice. Ego can be described as a force which both inspires you to cry as a baby (I WANT FOOD!), or which encourages self-centred attitudes at a later stage. The question is whether such attitudes (screaming for food/attention/quick reactions at the age of 50, for example) are still appropriate. This is where awareness should jump in to attempt to assess the situation. Often you will scour the past when searching for a solution to a conflict or issue in the present, but you must try and release this, otherwise your situation will not change. It is very beneficial to try and unhook yourselves from the "automatic" nature of your reactions. I wish everyone well on this voyage of discovery.

QUESTION ABOUT RELIGIOUS INFLUENCES

Dear Seraphin: when watching my own behaviour towards others who are behaving in an egoistic way, I often feel remorse when insisting on my personal rights. I think that my catholic education of always being good to others is wrong.

While educating children, I have learned a lot about the importance of being consistent. Sometimes I think that this is also necessary with adults. Would you please tell me where and how the old belief systems (especially education through Christian religion) is wrong, and how we can get a better understanding of our relationships to each other? How we can learn to protect our self-esteem without feeling remorse because we have refused something to others?

ANSWER FROM SERAPHIN

Greetings to you. You are in the process of learning how special and precious you really are. To be fully anchored in the DIVINE, and to have the certain knowledge that one is part of the DIVINE PLAN, plus the conviction that one is not placed onto this earth by chance but that it is your conscious decision in order to be of service - all this will cause you to carry yourself with ease, exuding an air of natural authority which it will be impossible to breech and which will command the respect of everyone you encounter.

This is this position which we urge you and all others to adopt in order to show the way for others. This is not a stance of being "egotistical": this is simply knowing your worth, and your value to the world. This is not insisting on personal rights; it is utilising every opportunity given to manifest your mission and to remove that which contradicts the path of your mission.

If your manner is firm as a result, so be it, for the significance of your journey is fully known to you, and it is regarded by you - ideally - as your main priority. If this involves "refusing" to comply with the demands or wishes of others, then so be it, for your sense that this is the right proceeding to enhance your path will OVERRIDE any feelings of "remorse" or regret.

This may sound rather harsh. Our aim here is to draw your attention to the STRAIGHTNESS OF YOUR PATH. If you allow others - well-meaning or not - to deter you from it, your pace will be slackened, and thus your joy in serving also.

If you observe others acting in an "egotistical way", this is something which you may observe IN YOURSELF. You can only perceive what you know from yourself. But regarding behaviour as "egotistical" is probably a relic from so-called Christian teachings which tend to teach SUBMISSIVENESS. We mean this in the sense that the expectancy instilled in you to be submissive may make you perceive anything contrasted to this behaviour as "egotistical".

So just continue observing your reactions to "egotistical" behaviour, and investigate whether this is really so, or if this is just the way it appears to you. Christian religions are "wrong" in the sense that they do not encourage independence, and they do not encourage the view of oneself as Divine.

Instead they present the Divine as a mighty outside presence which has to be OBEYED and which is only accessible through certain rituals and in certain places.

All these restrictions are imprisoning your minds,
and all these shackles shall fall.

QUESTION ABOUT HAPPINESS

Dear Seraphin: I have realized from the people I know around me, that despite their material possessions, they cannot reach what is called HAPPINESS.

These people are always keenly aware of lack - mostly material stuff - and almost always their EMOTIONAL BODY is suffering.

Seraphin, how can the emotional body be healed? Is it possible?

ANSWER FROM SERAPHIN

Greetings to you. We would like to say that "healing" is always possible, but that this is not some mystical or magical process initiated OUTSIDE OF YOURSELF. As we have mentioned a number of times, personal input and decisions are required from those in need of healing, especially the recognition of self-involvement. And HOW CAN YOU NOT BE INVOLVED IN HOW YOUR BODY IS OR HOW IT REACTS?

Your tendency on your earth to separate mind from body and the physical from the mental is a source of illness in itself, together with the derisive and scathing attitude towards all that is unseen. To put it in a simple way: if you set a goal, your feet will know which way to walk. If the goal is lacking, your walk will be directionless. If you feel like a victim and incapable of moving in any direction whatsoever, imprisoned in a cage from which you cannot escape, then the very idea of moving is like a very distant and unreachable and faint possibility.

This perspective does not exist for many ill people. They might put it all down to being "old", and thus all self-responsibility is dismissed. The same holds true for those who have emotional problems or relationship issues; they consider themselves to be afflicted by someone else, and then the removal of that person from their lives - letting them out of the enclosure into the great field of freedom - will be the solution. But this will not enable the setting of a new course. It merely frees up space for another person or circumstance to enter the arena and play the same game, for the behaviour has not changed and no new destination has been set.

What is your choice now, children of earth? Which destination will you choose? Do you choose to wallow in your self-concocted quagmires, or do you choose to pull yourselves out of it and survey it from a nearby hill? Will you restrict yourselves to the small cramped areas of thought and action and routine which make you feel "safe", or will you break out and see what is really going on here? Without stepping out, you cannot see. We plead with you to seek the HIGHER GROUND in all senses of the word.

SERAPHIN ANSWERS QUESTIONS ON PROBLEMATIC ISSUES

QUESTION ON CIVIL RIGHTS MOVEMENTS

Seraphin, please can you address what is going on in the USA with the Black Lives Matter Movement? This distresses me because we have experienced a great deal of growth in fact in the USA with black rights since the days of Martin Luther King, and many people work well together in the mix of white, black, Hispanic, Asian and Arabs.

ANSWER FROM SERAPHIN

We thank you for your question and sit in awe of your contribution to this world. And now for our answer. So many people presently incarnated on this planet are able to look into their past and find, in their memories, an unpleasant situation in which they DID NOT MATTER, in which they or their needs were overlooked, in which they were forced to accept the decisions of others to their own detriment, in which their position worsened, in which they were forced to struggle or suffer. In many of those cases, those who did not succumb actually turned to violence in order to defend themselves, to feed themselves, and to again look BIG in their own eyes and in the eyes of others.

It is no surprise, therefore, that these attitudes and this sort of behaviour – both the sad surrender and the "NOT MATTERING" as well as the tendency to erupt in anger and aggression so that one "matters" once again – is sown strongly into the genetic mind of your earth, seeding it with all manner of instructions which support both dependency and strife. This mind-set is reinforced and represented on earth in those now incarnated, and also (as a re-sult) in the genetic mind, and is available as such as instructions to all those who tend towards these mind-sets, supporting them in their thoughts and actions.

Certain nations and groups are stronger illustrations or manifes-tations of this, and so when the call goes out, the response is all the stronger. The call to MATTER AGAIN will reactivate those cells of memory, will appeal to centuries of memories of whole nations and groups who have systematically been downtrodden.

If you add to this the maze of propaganda sown into your sys-tems, and its widespread dissemination by the media under das-tardly control, then it results in a situation which is indeed very flammable. It can burst into flames at the mere whisper of "actu-ally, you matter".

While different groups may well work together in comparatively sane and clean and savoury and financially generous environ-ments, take away these elements and conflict is programmed.

You may find all colours and nations working together affably if the money is good, if all needs are provided for, and if it is in their own personal interest. High-level operations and charities are full of this sort of "internationality", but take away the high salaries and you would find very few of these working in such a way due to high principles or ideals alone.

Ironically, such employees are often desirous to work in such or-ganisations for the status they endow and BECAUSE THEY WANT TO MATTER.

True understanding and true friendship can only be found, and can only be discovered, through situations where money is not involved. True dedication is when the "costs" or "reward" are not the focus of the arrangement.

Do black lives matter?

The very question begs you to choose between two answers, yes or no. Polarisation by deliberate attempt has often been a method of division.

You are now moving towards the time when it will be clear to you all – through the chain reactions going on and the clear revelation of how all is connected – that EVERYTHING MATTERS.

To pull out just one section of the EVERYTHING is to forget the whole, is to look at the ground instead of the horizon. Broadening the horizons in every way should be the continual desire of those who are consciously seeking the light, who wish to transform, who wish to live in peace and who wish to contribute to this amazing process.

We thank you for this timely question and bow our heads deep in respect at the depth and quality and perseverance of your work. Seraphin

QUESTION ABOUT USING MEDITATION IN PRISONS

Seraphin: can prisoners who are convinced they have the right to rob and commit crimes be changed through Vipassana meditation or by any other method?

ANSWER FROM SERAPHIN

We greet the one who asks this question - one who is confronted with difficulties often and who is in dismay about the present prison population before his eyes. There are several aspects to be taken into consideration here.

One major concern is that many of these people, especially young people, are not aware of their own SIGNIFICANCE. Indeed, for most of their lives they have been told about their INSIGNIFICANCE, and this has fuelled their dissatisfaction, their unease, their sense of worthlessness.

Many also have been "trodden on" by higher authorities, or family members who were "stronger" than themselves, or who neglected them seriously.

To the question WHY ARE YOU IMPORTANT, they would not be very ready with answers, yet to cultivate this - that they have a definite purpose in life, and that they are unique in this, their life's mission - is something which is very important to distil and develop. They may well ask HOW IS IT POSSIBLE TO CULTIVATE THIS IN THESE VERY LIMITED SURROUNDINGS, in a prison?

The answer to that is:

BROTHERLY AND SISTERLY CONCERN
FOR FELLOW INMATES.
THERE IS ALWAYS A PLACE TO START.

SELF-IMPROVEMENT is also a key word in this scenario. The internal work which is so necessary may – in some more mature and reflecting inmates – be encouraged by some forms of meditation in their shorter forms. Vipassana is an extremely long version to which novices should not be thrown without previous experience. It is very easy to push some of these inmates "over the edge" as their levels of "frustration" are not very high.

With these it is better to start with physical exercises which are at the same time mental exercises – some forms of yoga and training exercises/martial arts/aikido come to mind here, as well as balancing exercises – which simultaneously help to train discipline, strength, holding out, and flexibility. And being able to "fall" easily. Falling (being "weak", when it can also mean being intuitive) is, in their minds, connected to something extremely negative.

What else do these people require to progress?

As always, it is LOVE.

This may be a completely foreign concept to them, depending on their various backgrounds, yet with good role models to demonstrate this, those with a "glimmer of hope" inside themselves, will eventually realise the power of love to uplift, and they may wonder at the results.

There will of course be those which will remain impervious to all these methods, who will refuse to reflect upon their behaviour, who will refuse to ask themselves questions, who will never write a diary about their feelings or realisations, and unfortunately, however much you increase your efforts, they will not change. These ones are destined to go elsewhere when the so-called "end times" come to a final halt.

We thank you for your work in this area – it has not gone unnoticed. You will become an excellent advisor, in the end, of how to deal with very difficult cases. Seraphin

QUESTION ABOUT SEXUAL ABUSE

Can you tell me, Seraphin, whether experiencing sexual abuse as a child will contribute to moving towards abusive behaviour in adulthood?

Can meditation help those who have abused or been abused?

ANSWER FROM SERAPHIN

We thank you for your question, which indeed throws up a whole series of MORE QUESTIONS, since this is a vast area on which several influences, trends and also physical issues all have their own effect.

The major concern, as we see it, is the issue of
MAJOR DEVIANT SEXUAL BEHAVIOUR.

The major question is:

HOW HAS IT EVOLVED THAT PEOPLE
TREAT EACH OTHER LIKE ANIMALS,
AND HOW DOES THE DESIRE
TO EXPLOIT OTHERS ARISE?

The crux of this physical problem – in that abuse is the physical manifestation - is actually a spiritual one. There are many definitions of spirituality – being in constant wonder and gratitude, regarding everything as holy, the concept that each of us has a task to fulfil to benefit humanity, the idea that "karma" will catch up with us one day, and the concept of a journey eternal in which we improve ourselves through spiritual growth, with the aim of attaining perfection.

Acts such as rape demonstrate the EXACT OPPOSITE of these principles, illustrating, in fact, a COMPLETE LACK of such principles. So you have to ask yourselves:

HOW DID THIS UNPRINCIPLED WORLD ARISE?

Did it just pervade the mental landscapes of the perpetrators? Was there any resistance? Was there any thought of what would happen, beyond the act itself? Was there no concept of

CONSEQUENCES OF ONE'S ACTION?

It is of course possible that being brought up in a culture of rape or other tendencies is going to produce same, out of rage, out of a desire to gain revenge, out of a desire to be the perpetrator instead of the victim JUST THIS ONCE. Or perhaps more than once. It may be hard for any victim of such events to see him or herself as worthy at all. It requires intense thinking and soul-searching from an OBJECTIVE DISTANCE in order to free oneself from unthinkingly carrying on certain behavioural patterns.

Work on oneself is always imperative, whatever one has experienced. If one has a complete understand of DIVINE TIMING, then all incidents exist for further learning, serving to WAKE UP OTHERS and WAKE UP SELF. This will be hard for many to hear, especially those who are the first to respond to victims who need help.

This is the first stage, yes, and it is very necessary, but there is a second stage where the question must be asked WHY ME? And WHAT CREATED THIS SITUATION?

The reasons may ostensibly be a distorted background, poverty, victimisation of all sorts, massive propaganda which weakens, or mind control which controls, but there is ALWAYS A PERSONAL

ELEMENT WHICH ALSO CONTRIBUTES. Having said this, it is difficult to generalise because each individual is on his or her own very individual path, with their own very individual choices of how to act or react or do nothing.

Concerning criminal acts, a criminal may benefit from prison, or meditation, or a period of time in service. Victims may also benefit from various forms of therapy, of which meditation may be one. It is best for each to choose – in the sense of free will – which method is suited to any particular moment (i.e. within their present context or situation) in order to raise their vibrations or – if the situation is very difficult – to clutch at a straw which will

SAVE THEIR LIVES.

This whole topic raises many questions; how deeply will people stoop before they claim their rights?

How much blood must flow before measures are implemented to stop it?

How many children have to be raped before completely different teachings on sex and spirituality are enforced in schools?

These are just a few of the questions which everyone should consider with respect to the rapidly degenerating moral standards in your societies.

We thank you for opening up a much-needed discussion on this very serious subject.

Seraphin.

QUESTION ABOUT REFUGEES

Seraphin: to what extent are refugees coming to Germany manipulated, especially the young men?

ANSWER FROM SERAPHIN

Greetings to you and thank you for enquiring after the young men who are travelling in their presently chosen role of "refugee".

This is a choice and a choice of role, as all others, to find the best way to GROW SPIRITUALLY.

To leave everything behind is the greatest challenge. Many of these "young men" are carrying an extra burden in the sense that they cannot leave their ideologies behind.

TO FAIL TO ADJUST AND TO FAIL TO LEARN IS TO BE IN A CONTINUAL STATE OF INNER AND OUTER CONFLICT.

This is their particular challenge – whether to deteriorate into violence – a reflection of the inner violence they are inflicting on themselves – or to gravitate towards LOVE. This is a time where all EXTREMES come to the foreground and when everyone is forced to CHOOSE.

Note also that many manipulative forces and propaganda are at work. They, and you also, are caught in a thick jungle of lies. This is the ultimate challenge of your times – TO STEP OUT OF THIS JUNGLE. In this, EVERYONE IS IN THE SAME BOAT, and, if I may say it, IN THE SAME REFUGEE BOAT. You are all seeking refuge from what you consider to be perverse, violent and inhumane systems, and to solve this, this, YOU MUST ALL BECOME GENTLE AND HUMANE. It is as simple as that.

Though many stories about "refugees" abound, and though many opinions are spreading, check yourselves continually for your own reactions and disorders, including overreactions. All your emotions of hatred and fear will enter the earth's genetic mind.

IS THIS YOUR INTENTION? Be scrupulous in your thoughts and intentions, as we have already indicated earlier. Be aware that you may see incidents or hear words which get your "shackles up". But know also that you may be mistaken. We would like to draw your attention to an incident related to this scribe by a friend who was undergoing a teacher-training course for service in Africa. She was told the following by her African colleagues: "Oh, you will have a lot of problems in Cameroon if you do not smile more. You just stand at the bus stop and say nothing. You do not even greet anyone." We leave you with this thought that so many of you are reticent and numb when faced with strangers, often pretending that they are not there. WELL, NOW THEY ARE THERE IN GREAT NUMBERS. SO, WHAT WILL YOUR OWN REACTION BE? As always, it is your choice. We are watching you and wish to support you. Seraphin

QUESTION ABOUT LGTB ISSUES

Dear Seraphin: on my island, society largely disdains LGTB behaviour and at times uses violence towards these people so as to contain them. At the same time, we have groups talking about human rights as thinly veiled attempts to manipulate the government to accept the practice of this behaviour. To what extent does the advent of porn and of manipulation by the media exacerbate this situation? What would be the best solution to approach and address this problem on this island?

ANSWER FROM SERAPHIN

Greetings to you, who often enters into territories unseen by the majority of the public. May you be the light of inspiration which provides hope.

That which is presented to the public eye is indeed very different from what you encounter, and what you perceive as truth. The media (as do other forces) are pouncing on all incidences of "deviance" in order to harass, divide and, ultimately, to control. This places you in a difficult position, with the demarcation line between disinformation and reality being clear to you. Your role in this is to cautiously enlighten – we say cautiously for pressures are at the moment extreme and are in fact fuelled by outward energies which are propelling the separation process. This period will not last forever. It will cumulate. And thus you can expect intense incidents involving hate and love, at both ends of the spectrum, as it were.

Concerning what is missing in your society generally; it is the feeling of compassion and respect. This is fuelled by fear and poverty. Seeing grave differences between yourselves and others results in fear and hatred. This is a loss of humanity which we are speaking of. This is decreasing rapidly, and as we said, any pretext will be taken and publicised and exaggerated for effect. The police will see it as their duty to keep order, as their orders are to crush all "dissidence", yet it is the political powers which decide what this term "dissidence" entails.

The general lesson to be learnt here is that the SIMILARITIES between people should be searched out, rather than various traits considered peculiarities. Love is not a peculiarity, irrespective of who offers it and who receives it. The problem with the gay and lesbian etc. agenda (and porn is certainly a powerful player in this scenario) is that the focus slips away from loving concern and concentrates on the sexual aspect. To love means to serve another, not to harm another. Destructive sexual practices, performed by whomever, is not offering love.

Your island is a melting pot for extreme behaviours. This scribe is seeing a society struggling to get by and struggling also to find some sense in their existence. This is a great challenge, and there will be those who can "rise to the occasion", so be on the lookout for these ones who are aware of the adversary and who will recognise you as a further step on their journey to more knowledge. This is what we can provide you with today. We honour your courage, Seraphin

QUESTION ABOUT PUTTING DOWN PETS

Dear Seraphin: it is my opinion that taking the lives of pets - even out of compassion - is still killing, as we cut off their life stream. On the other hand, we might want to end their suffering. Are we allowed to do this?

ANSWER FROM SERAPHIN

Greetings to you for your question. It shows the large discrepancy which lies between principles as they are stated, and principles as they are carried out. To value and respect all life is the principle. If this relates to a human being, a close relative who is visibly nearing the end of his or her life, for example, you may decide to place them in a hospice, to try and make their last days comfortable and valuable, to ease the pain of their "passing", to spend time together, to reassure, to do all that is possible.

How different, then, to give your animal to a vet - a person who has no relation with the animal - for an impersonal death. As with an incapacitated person, it is YOUR CHOICE and also YOUR RESPONSIBILITY what the quality of these final days should be. As always, the prime mover should be COMPASSION, and it is not our task to advise to what degree you should exercise this compassion, for this would remove your challenges and set us up as authorities when you yourselves should be developing your inner authority. Each case it different, and your task is to see how compassionately you may approach it.

QUESTION ABOUT THE LOSS OF A PET

Dear Seraphin. I would like to ask you how can I recover from the loss of my beloved dog. He died just after I had seen a rainbow. Was that a sign? Is there any connection?

ANSWER FROM SERAPHIN

Greetings to you, the Bereaved. The loss of a beloved pet is always very painful for those with love in their heart, such as that which you carry. Yet if the love runs deep, the pain will also be accompanied by joy because you will rest in the knowledge that your pet is at an immense stage of SOUL GROWTH, enabling it to CHOOSE CONSCIOUSLY and DETERMINE THE NEXT STEPS IN ITS PATH. This is their joy, and thus it should be your joy also. I can express no guarantees for future meetings, since this is subject to the free will choice of all parties concerned, yet where close bonds are forged they are not forgotten once "death" (which is the equivalent of "new life") has occurred. As with all things, thinking about something or someone will DRAW THEM NEAR in one way or another.

Concerning signs, such as rainbows in the sky or any other event which catches your attention, this is dependent on YOU as to whether your awareness is "online", so to speak. So many signs or helpful suggestions and indeed warnings are sent but not received because the antennae have not grown or have not been switched on.

We suggest that you (and here I mean you generally, pertaining to all on earth) increase your awareness of what is going on around you and try to reach a HIGHER LEVEL OF NOTICING while remaining steady. It is equally easy, if resting in a place of fear, to see signs in EVERYTHING and to conclude that they are ALL SIGNS OF FOREBODING.

This is a delicate but very exciting path to tread, ever learning about how your manifestation powers create your reality, and how angelic guidance ("signs") interacts with your creations. We wish you great progress in recognising this synergy effect and utilising it for the enlightenment of others.

QUESTION ABOUT DRUGS

Dear Seraphin: does Ayahuasca or do other drugs increase awareness, and to what extent are they harmful?

ANSWER FROM SERAPHIN

Greetings to you whose concern for the youth on our planet is so very great. If only everyone carried such deep concern, yet so many are concerned mainly with THEMSELVES and how to acquire the material goods which will make them feel secure, respected, admired. Yet this is not the aim or motivation which is ascribed to the evolving human being. What we mean is that

SPIRITUAL GROWTH has been all but smothered. The initial desire may have developed, yet it is ensnared and smothered as part of the deliberate machinations of those who wish to exert absolute power on your earth.

The subconscious knowledge and innate desire to grow sometimes remains, and thus such plants and drugs which supply this missing factor of A GROWING EXPERIENCE may appear to be very attractive, especially as some of these offer a change of perspective and mood at the drop of a hat.

Yet mostly, this is momentary and temporary, with many falling into the trap of material/money pursuit in order to repeat that "amazing" experience. This is a contradiction – pursuit of the material for the pursuit of the spiritual. What many have failed to see is that WHATEVER YOU DO IS AN EXPRESSION OF YOUR LEVEL OF SPIRITUAL GROWTH, and that these are not to be separated into two categories.

Spiritual growth is not something which can be facilitated by a bought substance. It is the result of self-effort over a long period of time. Easy quick fixes are nothing more than light relief and escape from a self-made reality. Until there is absolute acceptance that the unfavourable situation one finds oneself in is a RESULT OF PERSONAL ACTIONS TAKEN OR NOT TAKEN, then no substance will be able to remedy your plight on a permanent basis.

As with all experiences, drug-taking will offer opportunities to grow, even if it simply propels your decision – at some point along the line to be decided by yourself – to reject that particular path. (If you never reject, addiction is the consequence of that).

The only way to avoid this whole dilemma is to start education of the very young in a way which cements their knowledge of themselves as divine beings with limitless potential due to their ability to create their future. Knowledge of the Laws of Creation and Balance will help them to work IN ALIGNMENT with these laws, which play out irrespective of their acceptance of them or not, and to fully understand the infallible working of

CAUSE AND EFFECT.

There will perhaps be cries of YES, BUT IT MUST BE POSSIBLE TO EXPLORE EXCITING OTHER REALITIES. We would suggest that the most exciting thing you can do is to GET NEAR TO THE DIVINE IN MEDITATIVE MOMENTS where all answers and instructions are available. REAL COMMUNICATION with others, and developing real intimacy with others, is also a way to learn, to give and take, to form relationships of all kinds, instead of forming a relationship (and these are often harmful and addictive ones) with drugs.

How much more fulfilling will your lives be when you move onto these paths we describe, Beloveds? How much more will you be able to relate to others and thus to better assess how others can be assisted and LOVED IN TURN? In the end, there is only this: love. And the more you give, the more you will receive, as per the law of cause and effect. To perceive, instead, that you are in a state of lack and that some hole needs to be filled, and to use drugs to fill that hole, is leading to a negative downward spiral. To turn around and acknowledge abundance, and to give that to someone else, means that the love and abundance will return to you. I would advise anyone feeling down or suffering from depression to TRY THIS OUT. You can experiment with this. And don't forget to LOVE YOURSELVES.

QUESTION ABOUT THE EDUCATION SYSTEM

The education system is a mess in my country, Seraphin.
What can educators do?

ANSWER FROM SERAPHIN

Thank you for your question. Tell your students that they are wonderful, that they are an integral part of the Divine, that they are important in that each has a very specific task to fulfil on earth, determined even before incarnation, which also determined the setting and family circumstances in which the individual finds him or herself.

Tell them that this is a stage, and that they are the main protagonist, and that new scenes and new characters OF ONE'S OWN DEVISING AND WISH TO LEARN will enter the stage to test them, to encourage them, but above all, to encourage growth, maturity, and the acquiring of wisdom so that the mark they leave on this world, and the traces they leave behind, will be in alignment with the originally specified task.

Tell them that this is a self-chosen adventure.

Do not sympathise too much, but say:

HOW INTERESTING!
I WONDER WHAT YOU WILL CHOOSE TO DO NEXT?

Offer compassion but do not let it override everything else. And as educators, BE AND DEMONSTRATE THE EXHILARATION YOU EXPERIENCE DURING YOUR PURSUIT OF THIS SAME SPIRITUAL PATH. We thank you for your question as it is of extreme importance for the future balance of your world.

QUESTION ON EUTHANASIA

Dear Seraphin. This is a difficult topic. Is euthanasia under any circumstances ever ethical or justifiable? Can we assist with ending the life of a person in terminal suffering when all other avenues of assistance and attempted healing has been exhausted? Isn't this just simply another form of murder-suicide where man once again takes the decision of life or death in his own uninformed hands? Is this an issue where compassion should be restricted if it violates the Law of Life?

ANSWER FROM SERAPHIN

Greetings to you, and thank you for your great concern for LIFE. In the course of your question, you have actually provided the answer also. Yes indeed: in our eyes, euthanasia is another form of murder:

IT IS ENDING A LIFE-STREAM
WITHOUT BEING FULLY AWARE OF THE
ACTUAL MIND FRAME AND SPIRITUAL CONDITION
OF THE INDIVIDUAL CONCERNED.

In addition, ONLY THE PERSON CONCERNED - whether consciously or subconsciously or on a level not actually "known" to him or herself - CAN MAKE THE DECISIONS TO LEAVE. This will be a decision in conjunction with unseen advisors. IF WE CHOOSE TO DECIDE FOR THEM, this interrupts the process of CLOSURE - if this is actually the stage which the individual has reached. Consider that there are many people who care for the elderly. They will tell you that they can see when a certain person they are caring for HAS DECIDED to leave. This involves stopping eating and other signs. Then, they will say, it is only question of waiting for a while.

Concerning why shouldn't humans be euthanized out of compassion, as is the case with animals, this question is somewhat misplaced BECAUSE IT IS ALREADY COMMONPLACE IN YOUR INSTITUTIONS WHICH YOU CALL HOSPITALS. MANKIND SHALL NOT TAKE LIFE AND DEATH INTO ITS OWN HANDS. MANKIND MUST LEARN TO RESPECT LIFE IN ALL ITS FORMS. MANKIND SHOULD NOT EXTEND LIFE ARTIFICIALLY OR END IT ARTIFICIALLY. MAN SHOULD NOT INTERFERE WITH PROCESSES WHICH HE OR SHE VIEWS FROM A VERY INCOMPLETE AND LIMITED PERSPECTIVE.

Know that everyone - in whatever health condition - is attended by guides and helpers in the unseen realms who aid transition. IT IS NOT MAN'S PRIVILEGE TO DO SO.

WE ARE NOT SAYING NO MORE PAINKILLERS:
WE ARE SAYING
NO MORE INTERFERENCE AND
NO MORE LACK OF RESPECT FOR THE VERY
LIFE-STREAMS OF WHICH YOU YOURSELVES ARE PART.

Can you see where this may go? Imagine that it is pronounced "ethical" to end the life of someone with a so-called terminal disease at eighty. What about someone who has a disease at 79, or at 50? MAN DOES NOT MAKE THESE RULES, AND YOU WILL REAP THE CONSEQUENCES OF SUCH ACTIONS, AS IN THE LAW OF CAUSE AND EFFECT.

This is a good opportunity to look at something which is very important. Take a good, long, hard look at all the things you do not say because you think that it is better to SPARE ANOTHER PERSON THAT PARTICULAR TRUTH OR EXPERIENCE.

In condoning euthanasia, you are not only cutting off their life, YOU ARE CUTTING OFF THEIR EXPERIENCE. By holding your tongue, you may prevent someone from being hurt, but also you prevent them from KNOWING THE TRUTH.

How can you know the truth of what is going on in a person's mind, and how can you determine whether that life is worth living or not? It is not for you to judge. It is for the person themselves to judge.

QUESTION ON HOMOSEXUALITY

Dear Seraphin: we know that if a soul is to become well balanced it needs to experience many facets of being in order to understand and grow wisdom. This includes the experiencing of life in the body of both genders so that it can come to understand both sides of that existence and balance out the male and female energies within itself.

In relation to this my question is: What motivates homosexuality and why can some people not come to terms or understand why they are in one gender's (like a male) body while they feel the opposite and different inside (like a female) and vice versa for females with some even going as far as changing their physical bodies?

What can the reasons for this type of inclination and behaviour be on a deeper level other than the known suppositions of genetics, environment, so-called "gender confusion" or just something like a failed relationship which turns some people off from the other gender and causes them to seek the affections of their own gender? Thanks for any clarification on this.

ANSWER FROM SERAPHIN

Greetings to you. Balance is one of the most importance qualities for the health of an individual soul, as for the wellbeing of your planet. Your earth will, in fact, be entering a phase during which her rebalancing will be of primary importance, and you will similarly and simultaneously be asked to cleanse yourself of any imbalances, whether this is exaggerated behaviour, exaggerated focus on unimportant aspects, or unbalanced reactions to whatever catalysts come into your view to be experienced.

The origins for being sexually attracted to one person rather than to another are myriad and can include one or more of the aspects you have already mentioned. What we cannot emphasise enough here is the UNIQUE NATURE AND EXPERIENCE OF EVERY INDIVIDUAL SOUL, INCLUDING ALL PREVIOUS INCARNATIONS AND ALL UNSOLVED "KARMA", INCLUDING ALL MOTIVATIONS AND INTENTIONS STATED PREVIOUS TO THE CAREFUL SELECTION OF CIRCUMSTANCES OF THIS INCARNATION. In this, nothing is left to "chance": the variations occur in accordance with the choices made when facing these circumstances. In general, we would like to say:

THERE IS TOO MUCH ATTENTION PAID
TO THE SEXUAL ASPECT OF YOUR LIVES.

This may sound quite simple and indeed it is quite simple. To focus upon differences and discuss differences at great length and to express shock at perceived great differences means the INCREASE IN DIVISION AND STRIFE which is the DESIRED CONDITION PERPETRATED BY YOUR SLAVE MASTERS.

And again, the simple answer is:
STRAIN TO ACHIEVE BALANCE AND FOCUS ON LOVE AS

A PRIORITY. TO LOVE SOMEONE IS NOT TO HURT THEM. The main issues here is that anal sex practices are physically DAMAGING (This is another aim of your slave-masters: to reduce the quality/health of the material body)

NO ONE WHO REALLY LOVES SOMEONE ELSE WOULD INDULGE IN THIS ACTIVITY, IRRESPECTIVE OF SEX.

To provide a wider perspective: when you proceed as a soul along the paradise journey, it is specially arranged that you encounter a variety of different souls in different bodies which may, at the beginning, appear to be quite astounding to you. With increasing contact and familiarity, however, friendships are formed and similarities found. This is a part of celestial training, and this earth is certainly a good learning ground for this also.

Imagine you see a person in the distance who you consider to be THE EXACT OPPOSITE OF YOURSELF in every way - physical mental and spiritual. Let that person approach you in your mind's eye and look into their eyes for a long time. Then talk to each other about your deepest concerns and desires. Try and form a bond. This will happen despite differences if both really want to connect. Do not be put off by differences or fall into fear due to differences, for this is how conflicts arise and how wars are provoked. We know that we are taking a big perspective here, but we think it essential to present this aspect in a much wider context than that which is normally considered. Consider also that there are beings who incorporate all male and female aspects, and that there are also beings who are "hermaphrodites" on other inhabited planets. If contemplating this, you will see that there is a completely different slant to such a question. We thank you for this opportunity to teach.

QUESTION ABOUT YOUNG PEOPLE AND JOBS

Dear Seraphin. In our world, there are so many young people who cannot find a job, some because they are living in countries where the economy is down, others because they are studying at universities where a lot of them fail at the exams. Some of them would be better off with more manual or practical work, but at least in the Western world, this is not held in good esteem. Nor is it well paid. What can we do to encourage our children and young people to choose a profession where they can find fulfilment and thus fill this world with joy and not with frustration?

ANSWER FROM SERAPHIN

Greetings to you. Your concern for the fate of your young people is commendable since they are indeed on the wrong tracks - tracks which have been laid down carefully in order to ensnare them (AND ALL OF YOU). Once one finds oneself on these tracks, it is difficult to assert oneself and get off, and even more difficult to admit THAT ONE WAS RIDING THE WRONG TRAIN. It is very easy to follow a certain "career" or "expectation" if it is laid down before you. Every effort is made to push young people into avenues where they are easily controllable. This includes their dependence on money. Earning money is presented as THE ANSWER TO ALL PROBLEMS, whereas it is actually THE SOURCE OF ALL PROBLEMS. To eradicate it from your society completely would mean a great spiritual upsurge, living as communities who do nothing but CONTRIBUTE and SHARE evenly.

Wisdom and experience is not on a par with a university degree. This can only be gained through your OWN EXPERIENCE AND LEARNING PROCESSES. Of course, it is beneficial to study in certain areas, and much information can be gained, but it is the

PRACTICAL IMPLEMENTATION of this which proves to you whether this is a RELEVANT, POSITIVE and EFFECTIVE field of study which BENEFITS ALL.

As you live in human forms, the human aspect which involves movement, bodily functions and relating to each other on a physical level in a physical world, is paramount. It is not enough to philosophize and remove oneself from those who you may consider to be on a "lower" intellectual level, or to move only in certain "higher" level of society. Ideally, practical skills will be part of future schooling.

Apart from the useful aspect of such acquired prowess, this encourages also the feeling of self-worth of the students. They can see the RESULTS of their learning as translated into the physical. They are appreciated for what they produce and how they contribute. They learn the joy of co-creation and the joy of celebrating the success of joint projects. They can also SEE that they have had a positive effect on the WHOLE, instead of beavering away by themselves, in constant competition and in constant fear of others. It is not by chance that young people today feel discouraged and at a loss in the system they find themselves in. The system must be changed and the focus of educational institutions must be changed. Destruction of old systems of thought and the introduction of new information should revolutionise this in the near future.

Concerning fulfilment, this is found by young people when they DISCOVER THEIR REAL DIVINE VOCATION and their usefulness to others. To be in service is the greatest joy. Following WHAT ONE REALLY WANTS TO DO and LETTING YOUR ENTHUSIASM LEAD YOU ALONG YOUR CHOSEN PATH means that EVERY DAY IS LOOKED FORWARD TO, instead of counting the days till the weekend begins.

Why is it, Beloveds, that so many people in your world have depressions on Monday mornings? In this new, renewed world we are presenting you with here, this will be a phenomenon of the past. Neither will unemployment ever be a problem again. Each will have the RESPONSIBILITY to search out something which will contribute to everything working like the many cogs of a great machine. Employment and unemployment are words which it would be good to strike from your normal vocabulary. We favour "contribution" and "vocation" and "service". Imagine that you are asked this question: "WHAT SERVICE DO YOU PERFORM?" instead of "WHAT JOB DO YOU DO?" This is the new slant we would like to put on your present "working" lives.

QUESTION ABOUT OUR MAD WORLD

Dear Seraphin:

As far as I can see, ours is a sad world. I realized a long time ago that something on earth was going wrong. I am supposed to be living in a democracy, but every criticism you make of the 'leaders' will get you a night in jail or at least some form of financial litigation. I tend to be very empathetic towards other people, but sometimes I feel helpless trying to explain, because people are so brainwashed. They cannot be convinced.

I have difficulties convincing people that I am not mad. Many negative processes have started. What are we waiting for now?

ANSWER FROM SERAPHIN

Greetings to you. We can sympathise with you that you sense this is a "sad place to be in". You describe aptly some of the machinations which weigh the planet down and which, in fact, make it impossible for her to continue in this way in the long run. Action must be taken, by Gaia (your earth) with any assistance she may require.

To see the world as purely "sad" is, however, an inadequate description. Your lives are full of so many different nuances of feeling if only you open yourselves up to the ECSTASY which is possible for you, if only you REALLY WAKE UP TO THE WONDERS OF CREATION, starting off at a very near and familiar place, YOUR OWN BODIES. To feel, to smell, to sense, to move, to laugh, all these are joyous occurrences.

Do not delve so deep into the "sad" aspects of the staged performances surrounding you that you lose track of the TRUTH, THE JOY, THE LOVING REACTIONS BETWEEN MEN AND WOMEN IN ALIGNMENT WITH EACH OTHER AND WHO FOLLOW IMPORTANT PATHS AND STRIVE FOR IMPROVEMENT.

This is the danger: that excessive lamenting and occupation with the "dark side" - including the tendency to bite like a wounded dog whenever such themes are breeched - WILL FURNACE THE FUEL OF THE DARK SIDE. We commend you for seeing that something is "wrong". By now, many will have come to the same conclusion. Whether those have also concluded that this situation has something to do with themselves, and that their thoughts and actions are part of this, is another question entirely.

The challenge is to GO BEYOND the feeling of shock and horror, and assess it from a point of view which involves one's OWN

ROLE PLAYED ON THE DARK PATH. EVERYONE HAS TAKEN PART IN THIS IN SOME WAY, and we make no excuses for mentioning this. EVERYONE MUST UNDERSTAND THAT JOINT ACTION HAS RESULTED IN THIS. It is not just some vague result of intangible fleeting destructive forces with no name or structure. And you are playing out your lives WITHIN THESE STRUCTURES, which automatically involves your participation.

While the realisation that something is wrong is major, the realisation that you yourselves have participated in it is even more MAJOR. The awakening process, once started, is like peeling layer after layer off an onion. Again and again you will discover that something you considered to be true and well intentioned will turn out to have ulterior motives behind the pleasant facade. The souls who intend to pursue the upward journey will go through a WHOLE SERIES of such realisations, in fact, this will NEVER STOP as the soul wishes to follow a path of learning and ever greater refinement of his or her behaviour so that they are ever more increasingly attuned to the Laws of Balance.

You mention that you have difficulty convincing others that you are not mad. This is of little importance, and it is not your mandate to destroy yourself while trying to convince others against their will. Try to see the statement of "they cannot be convinced" not as a complaint, in the sense that they really ought to be convinced but refuse to be so, but regard it more like a completely neutral statement of fact: THEY CANNOT BE CONVINCED. This is because they do not have the antennae at this stage in events. You cannot force them to develop such. Prefer to conserve your energy for that which IS POSSIBLE.

You ask: what are we waiting for now? As said many times:

TIME IS MEANT TO BE USED WISELY AND
CONSTRUCTIVELY IN ORDER TO RAISE YOUR OWN
CONSCIOUSNESS AND TO FURTHER
YOUR OWN SENSE OF BALANCE.

PRACTICE BEING CENTRED IN THE MIDDLE OF CHAOS.

For this, you cannot practice too much. Time is not for waiting. This is a huge operation in front of us. The logistics are enormous. Please leave it at that. If you find that you are impatient of distrusting of the process, connect within often. And use each moment to ask yourself how you can contribute to the furthering of your own sense of sovereignty, and how you can contribute. Whether on earth or no, whether on ship or no, whether on another planet or whether in another body or incarnation, the question will always be the same:

HOW CAN YOU BEST CONTRIBUTE TO THE SOCIETY
IN WHICH YOU ARE LIVING TO MAKE IT A PEACEFUL
AND MORE PLEASANT PLACE TO LIVE

To follow such is never to have a moment of boredom. To do such is to be fulfilled beyond all that you have experienced before. Travel this road, dear friend, and we will walk with you.

QUESTION ON ARTIFICIAL INTELLIGENCE

Dear Seraphin: what help can we expect from celestial observers of our planet? Will they provide us with artificial intelligence in order to clean up the mess on earth and to "free up" time to develop the human mind and increase creativity?

ANSWER FROM SERAPHIN

Greetings to you. The presence of extra-terrestrial groups on your earth has a very long and varied history which would be difficult to express in its entirely here in a short synopsis. Several have been carrying ill-intent. Others have demonstrated intense curiosity, hoping to gain something from the human experience which might of use for their own species. Yet others have been entirely beneficial. They carry many names and numbers and are not to be the subject of discussion here. Be aware that there is also a great deal of misinformation available concerning the supposed activities of such groups.

The focus here is THE EVOLVEMENT OF HUMAN MIND, to be continued at a pace where all can move forward together. This means walking at the pace of the slowest, so that no-one is left behind. This is in fact exactly WHY the pace is now set to quicken, since those with a slow or stationary rate of spiritual development will not be able to keep up and will thus walk at a slower pace elsewhere. This impetus will make a whole range of new experiences possible, and will enable a whole range of new technology to be implemented which would have otherwise been used as weaponry by those who are of lower consciousness and little scruple.

This is your exact situation now, in fact. Artificial intelligence in its widest sense means that you can "entrust" certain activities to a computer which thinks for itself and which is capable of making decisions. Eventually, such "brains" - IN THE RIGHT HANDS - can also develop consciousness. So, a high level of spiritual thinking is necessary before such technology is allowed. To what degree (and how fast) this progresses depends essentially on how quickly earth inhabitants can "learn the new ropes", and how quickly the quality of LOVING THY NEIGHBOUR as an absolute and complete concept can be grasped and applied. Once understood and implemented worldwide, use of computers and "machines with minds" can be introduced and further developed without any danger. Rest assured that there are teams which oversee this whole operation.

QUESTION ABOUT PREDATORY ANIMALS

Seraphin: how will a higher vibration on earth affect animals, especially with regard to their predator/ prey relationships? Will the animals that remain also change over time to no longer needing to eat each other? We have seen animals in news stories who should have these predator/ prey relationships, and yet they become friends, so I know something is afoot in that regard already to some degree.

ANSWER FROM SERAPHIN

Greetings to you. Much of what you surmise is along the right lines. With the increase in vibration on the earth, all living beings including animals will be affected and will in fact have to "move" with it. This means that some species may not be able to remain on earth due to their very strong streak of aggression. The progress of animals means the progress of their souls, or group souls in the case of those like ants or lizards which have not individuated. They are further down the ladder than your cats and dogs who, due to their close contact with humans, are almost capable of developing consciences and capable of exercising choice. It is this ability to choose - between right and wrong, and knowing that the choice will bear consequences - which is lacking in the group souls.

Let us say that the SPEED at which this learning can take place will increase on the new earth. Humans, as creatures who can and do choose, chose not to eat each other if they have progressed long enough along the learning path. This is something which animals will follow. The present day free roaming cats which prey on others although they do not need to eat is one of the sad reflections of how you humans have distorted your own appetites, using and devouring resources which you DO NOT NEED. Cats imitate humans, and this is the result of that energy which destroys for no reason. Many humans of little conscience pour their thoughtless behaviour into earth's collective mind, for others to access. It is expected that those who remain on earth will attempt to be shining examples for your animals to follow.

QUESTION ON DEALING WITH TRAUMA

Dear Seraphin: could you please teach us how to deal with trauma? There are many people (adults and children) who have suffered physical and emotional abuse and cannot overcome the sadness and fear. I would like to know if there is something we need to learn from such experiences in order to be wiser.

ANSWER FROM SERAPHIN

My greetings to you, and thank you for bringing up this topic. The trauma experienced by individuals is - and this must be made very clear - the consequences of their actions in combination with a failure to learn spiritual principles. The "trauma" - in whatever form that might show itself - is the SYMPTOM of an experience - however unpleasant – which has not been processed. There are individuals on your world who have suffered a great deal of unpleasant experiences - including loss of family members - who have COME THROUGH IT ALL SHINING. These are souls who KNOW that this is not the end, and who KNOW that they are the creators of the next step in their lives and whose inner strength and knowledge of life processes and development always act as an INNER COMPASS WHICH STEERS THEM TOWARDS THE NEXT VALUABLE EXPERIENCE.

Another aspect of this is that traumatic events - if so traumatic that the memory of such would disturb the life-stream creativity - are suppressed by the memory in order to "wait" for a time when this particular soul can deal with it. This means that a memory may resurface after many years at a point where the person is in a position to process it. For those dealing with persons in trauma, this may seem like information which is very irrelevant to the depth of misery so obviously felt by their patients. Yet putting these patients through a programme in which their potential and creativity - with every thought and word - is furthered and sup-ported, including outpourings of continuous love vibration, will have stupendous effect.

What is a "continuous love vibration", one may ask? Not very many people on your earth are familiar with this: perhaps they may experience this when they fall deeply in love with someone and spend two weeks alone with them at a beautiful location. This is what you call "holiday" also, but which should be the vibration of EVERY HOLY DAY.

Living continually in an atmosphere where EVERYONE LOVES EVERYONE ELSE cannot fail to be healing. It is not enough to give weekly "therapy" sessions to children or adults who have suffered, for the SPACES IN-BETWEEN are not covered. There are so many methods of encouraging love and overcoming separateness. CONTINUOUS HOLISTIC TREATMENT is the answer. And this includes a great deal of spiritual teaching. How many of you are held, physically, in love every day? (AND HERE WE DO NOT MEAN SEX). This is what everyone - not only children - need every day. This is a basic human need, but your world has CUT ITSELF OFF FROM THIS. To be "cool" (as opposed to warm and embracing) is held as the highest compliment. It is time to build such an environment where love dominates, and in a world like this, emotional abuse can never arise.

QUESTION ABOUT TEEN SUICIDES

In South Africa, there have recently been a couple of high profile child/teen suicides. One was a 12-year-old girl who shot herself after deliberately planning it all for at least 3 months in advance and another was a 14-year-old girl who jumped to her death from a parking garage roof. In both cases mentioned the children hid their intentions from their parents until it was too late. These are only two cases among many which occur annually worldwide. Could you perhaps shed some light on why these children would commit these deeds (aside from obvious causes like being lonely or bullied which in itself is a huge problem for young people or feeling there is no future for them in their current life) and what can one say to the parent of such a child who got caught by surprise by these actions and are in inconsolable grief?

ANSWER FROM SERAPHIN

Greetings to you. Your great concern for these little ones shines through your words and through this question. While some may explain these suicides through causes such as bullying and other serious abuses, this is often only a symptom of what is really going on here. Such children with heightened awareness may have very great difficulty in adjusting to this very difficult earth plane, involving conditions and behaviours which seem irreparable and all pervasive. Sensitive souls which suddenly find themselves in such a deep pool of insensitivity and wrath, pervaded with negative emotions and intent, will struggle to swim for an allotted amount of time, according to their ability to endure.

Such souls were well aware of this challenge before incarnating, yet their real experience of being here went far beyond their expectations or imaginings - thus the desire to "try this out". Some do succeed in surpassing this and go on to become great fighters against the system. Their voices will become ever stronger as the changes are upon you.

Others never surface from the murky waters. Yet this also is a catalyst for change, notably for their parents and family who - through deep shock and grief, are in their turn forced to question and also to research how it could come to be that their child wished to depart from them, despite deep love. It is also a sign of deep love on the part of the child that he or she should decide to take this step. It is a desperate step, designed to wake those they love to the very great seriousness of the situation here on earth. This is not a final step, as their relatives may fear, but an interim strategy to propel and lift the level of consciousness.

One step always leads to another. Children who leave in this way are merely moving onto the next step of the same stairway. This means that family members will meet again - just as they have met again in this particular incarnation - because they are closely associated and ON THE SAME STAIRWAY, even if there are breaks in the journey, or deviations in the journey.

To such grieving parents I would say this; your child dealt with the situation as best they could, and you will meet again in different circumstances. Love is never lost. To hold someone in your memory in love is a vibration which will travel the universe, where the lost love resides. I thank you for your question.

QUESTION ABOUT MONEY

Money is a great need in my present situation, Seraphin. I am having difficulties manifesting money. Sometimes I am on the receiving end of money bills magically appearing. What can I do to increase it?

ANSWER FROM SERAPHIN

Greetings to you. It seems that you have been on the "receiving end", or so you perceive, for a considerable part of your life, whether these are pleasant or not so pleasant experiences. Now you describe that you are on the "receiving end" of money bills which appear - almost by magic - in front of you.

Magic is however something which people IMAGINE is happening, whereby there are actually UNSEEN REASONS OR EVEN UNSEEN ANGELS OR EVEN YOUR UNCONSCIOUS SELF putting the steps in-between, which would make this seem like a normal step by step procedure as opposed to a miraculous one.

Your personal unseen guides are not "money angels". But they are very interested in you experiencing ABUNDANCE in all senses of the word, and they create conditions which can help you reach the state of abundance. This tends to be in the form of CREATING OPPORTUNITIES FOR YOU, whether this is through a monetary windfall, or whether it is through another method which will result in abundance.

What you can rely upon is that they will also BLOCK paths you are taking which will result in the opposite. Above all, it is your SPIRITUAL WELFARE which your guides have at heart, and this is independent of what physical situation you may find yourself in at the moment.

In general, it can be said that a rich inner life - involving reflection, awareness, and being prepared to be flexible and creative - will enable abundance (also in the sense of material wealth) in your outer physical life. This means that your chosen ACTIONS will have more influence that contemplating a bank note for a long time.

I would also like to draw your attention to your statement "MONEY IS A NEED FOR MY SITUATION".

Please note the immense power of your words. What you state has tremendous influence. If you state emphatically that you are in a state of need, then such a statement will cement you into that situation and into that need.

If, by comparison, you make a statement like "May all the abundance coming to me enable me to further my mission in the service of humankind", you can imagine that this will have a VERY POSITIVE IMPACT ON YOUR SITUATION.

We are excited to see your presence on this forum, and the honest way in which you express yourself here. We see potential in your path for aiding others who will require a great deal of assistance in understanding how they can change to increase not only their happiness, but also that of others.

QUESTION ON BORDERS

Seraphin, I am interested to know whether present borders will remain on the new earth?

ANSWER FROM SERAPHIN

Greetings to you. The word "fluid" comes to mind when reading your question. Due to changes in coastline and at main rupture points in the earth's surface, there will be a serious change in borders caused by these events.

Yet people will still hold onto what they consider to be their "nationality", based also on the common language they may share.

With a vastly reduced population and - initially - reduced travelling capacities, the issue of where a border is will not be the greatest focus however.

Borders are presently a means of separation, and your focus in future will be that of co-operation and unity. Whether a border previously existed in a certain area and whether it will continue to exist will be irrelevant.

Great effort will be made to see that all people in a specific area have the conditions they need to survive and thrive.

Your present situation of many refugees attempting to cross borders in search of a "better life", whatever their understanding of that is, will cease.

You can rest assured that there will be the "right" leaders at the helm to facilitate this.

SERAPHIN ANSWERS QUESTION ON SPIRITUAL ISSUES

QUESTION ABOUT OUR TASK ON EARTH

Seraphin: I have been told that before we are born there is a list of tasks to achieve in our life time, and that if we don't succeed, we will keep reincarnating until we do. Due to all the complexities of life in general, we might lose track of these tasks. How, in later life, can we know what to do? You may say "go within", but I don't get answers easily, so is there any other way of knowing?

ANSWER FROM SERAPHIN

Greetings to you, who are SO MUCH GREATER THAN YOU PRESENTLY PERCEIVE. We do not mean this in the sense of material power as an overlord, but in spiritual stature.

What is agreed upon before birth is a preliminary template, a sketch, a bag of tricks or potential, a general setting. Requesting the help of your unseen helpers can assist you to move along a path which furthers your learning and your capabilities. Without recognition of them, and without specific requests for assistance, these steps cannot be realised because helpers do not interfere with free will. The result of being CONTINUALLY LINKED TO THE DIVINE WITHIN is in fact this "spiritual" stature which will automatically attract those who sense that you have something very valuable to GIVE, from which they will greatly benefit. Another reason for not finding one's true path or task is because your minds cannot conceive of your own greatness (and here we also address EVERYONE reading here). We would recommend in meditation that you imagine yourselves being crowned a "spiritual king or queen" and then visualise yourselves as advisors to those who are at a different place on the spiritual road. The prerequisite for this is, of course, your purity of motive to assist humanity in the very, very difficult situation it finds itself in, and which indeed humanity has itself created over thousands of years. Humility is also a prerequisite of spiritual greatness.

Put yourselves in this position of all-powerful assistance, aided by unseen angelic supporters, providing wisdom for all who seek it. This will cause you to examine closely your present capabilities, and with this added perspective that YOUR HORIZON IS LIMITLESS, your true task will evolve. You must suspend disbelief for a moment that this is all there is, that the situation is so overwhelming, that it is impossible to find a way out or to have a lasting effect. It may feel like knocking your head unnecessarily against the wall or barely making a dent in mind-sets which are so very much influenced by propaganda put out for many years.

But we say: do not concentrate on this aspect but on the possibilities and on your POTENTIAL WHICH HAS NOT YET BEEN EXPLOITED OR IMPLEMENTED. This is where your talent for visualising will also come in very useful. Your planet requires the relentless dedication of visionaries so that it can rise from its knees and move towards the state of "light of life" which – for those unfamiliar with this term – is the paradise state where everyone prospers and everyone contributes and where all behaviour is of the highest integrity. We hope we have been able to deliver words to you which will inspire, and we encourage you to expand your expectations of yourself along these lines. Our scribe will add an appropriate quote she has come across recently. Seraphin.

"Your whole idea about yourselves is borrowed from people who don't know themselves" (Osho)

QUESTION ABOUT ALL THINGS BEING REVEALED

Dear Seraphin. Many "holy books" have stated that all things will be revealed". Will they be revealed in dreams?

Will all unpleasant revelations be made public?

Does it depend on the severity of the offense?

Might revelations just take place between two individuals?

ANSWER FROM SERAPHIN

We thank you for your serious considerations of processes which are – as we speak – of increasing importance. Revelations are happening moment by moment, illuminating the field of knowledge of individuals as well as groups on all levels. Essential to realise is that nothing can be revealed to those who do not open their eyes, so those with open attitudes and a searching mind will be presented with "revelations" every day, as on a plate. It will be their daily "bread and butter". Others may drop their fear and investigate one day, only to shut down and reject their newly acquired knowledge the next. Such are the ups and downs, resulting in much confusion for others around them, at this particularly intense period in the history of your planet.

If knowledge is not accepted, and if veritable barriers are up against the acquisition of TRUTH, then indeed the Divine hand will find other ways to approach this problem, and dreams may be one way of approaching matters from a very different angle. There are actually so many methods of self-discovery and ways of "reframing" present situations in the light of more expansive perspectives, and if these are pursued, revelations will happen often. The bottom line is:

YOU DICTATE THE PACE,
ALTHOUGH THERE IS A COSMIC WIND BLOWING
WHICH WILL INCREASE THE PACE,
IRRESPECTIVE OF WHETHER YOU ARE WALKING
FORWARDS OR BACKWARDS.

The resulting conflict between those walking forwards and those walking backwards FUELS THE FIRE OF REVELATION, as many more facts are exposed as a result, like putting truth into SHARP RELIEF against a background of trivia and absurdity. All this serves to wake you up, children of earth.

This is a purely personal journey for all, for all personal journeys form the collective JOURNEY. In that sense, anything you do will affect the whole. In that sense, it is impossible for you to do something, or do something as "only two individuals", which does not affect the whole. Similarly, if anything is "revealed" to only two people, or between two people, it will still have an effect.

Those who pose questions, such as you, are to be commended. Those who continue stubbornly on their present unknowing path will only be provided with a revelation at the very end, which unfortunately may be too much to bear since the truth is EXACTLY THE OPPOSITE OF EVERYTHING THOUGHT SO FAR.

Concerning the "severity of the offence", the repercussions are downgraded if sincere repentance is sought. This is part of the learning journey which is so important. We are no longer in the days when the crime is received in exactly the same form as that committed by the perpetrator.

Yet the law of CAUSE AND EFFECT IS ALWAYS IN PLAY so that learning processes can continue.

The intent of any individual is the precursor of action, thus it is a powerful indicator to set your intent, yet without following it up, or taking action to ensure progress, intent alone will not bring you your desired outcome. Part of that process is to be aware, constantly, of opportunities put at your disposal. If you wish to receive information in the form of a dream, for example, it is best to pen your questions in a notebook at the side of your bed, and to ask your INNER DIVINE CORE what you need to know in this regard, and to WRITE DOWN what you remember when you awake, and to REPEAT this procedure several times, since some meanings are only grasped when seen in a series of dreams.

In such cases YOU are the person who concludes what SIMILARITIES or RECURRING TRUTHS they provide.

We hope that we have been able to provide you with some answers to your questions. Seraphin.

QUESTION ABOUT BEING UNIQUE

Seraphin: why does my uniqueness set me apart from others?

ANSWER FROM SERAPHIN

Why do you ask this question? Because you are not yet fully aware of your full creative capabilities and because you do not yet fully trust the process in which you are the main protagonist in all things great and in all things small. To walk in great awareness of this is to see signs ALL ALONG THE WAYSIDE. You would be in complete and continual communication with all things around you. Then there would be no need to ask the way. Why are you so unique? BECAUSE YOU ALL ARE. The state of being unique is universal. It is one of life's great challenges to recognise that everyone is unique, and to treat them as such. If you consider that other people are boring and uncommunicative and disinterested and not worth your time of day, and are somehow "below" your level of uniqueness, then there is indeed little possibility of friendships developing. Friendships rest on 50% communication and respect and effort on both sides. For your own "uniqueness" to be accepted, your challenge is to accept the "uniqueness of others" and refrain from making judgements about what or how you think they are. Note that everyone is in a continual state of flux, including yourself. What one person may consider boring today may be tomorrow's fascination, and vice-versa.

QUESTION ABOUT RESPONSIBILITY FOR DEATH

Seraphin: to what extent am I responsible for the death of my child, or was it the soul's decision to leave?

ANSWER FROM SERAPHIN

Greetings to you. We hold you in high regard. Though you do not know us intimately, we know of you and your challenges which – for the purpose of great and rapid learning – you have invited into your experience, in close consultation with all those involved (and this, by the way, can be said of all souls striving to follow the spiritual path and striving to improve themselves). For this we commend you.

It is important to remember that the human mind, locked as it is into the human body, does not have the same ability or capacity as the GOD MIND WHICH KNOWS ALL THOUGHTS AND WHICH KNOWS THE SOURCE OF ALL ACTIONS. THE GOD MIND UNDERSTANDS EVERY LAST DETAIL OF ALL SITUA-

TIONS, SO YOU ARE COMPLETELY UNDERSTOOD RE-GARDING YOUR MOTIVES, AND THAT IS WHY YOU ARE AL-WAYS COMPLETELY FORGIVEN.

Do not, any of you here on earth, torture yourselves with the idea that the DIVINE DOES NOT UNDERSTAND.

Neither is it helpful to think that the DIVINE HAND WORKS IN AN UNFAIR OR ARBITRARY WAY.

Its way is PERFECTION, and it is your limited perspective which judges otherwise.

Therefore, be in peace, and remember also that serious situations such as yours are PART OF THE PLAN, as blessed by prior discussion and decision BY ALL PARTIES INVOLVED.

It is hard NOT BEING ABLE TO REMEMBER THIS, yet all actions and events are ultimately steered by LOVE FOR YOU and the desire to ASSIST YOU ON YOUR JOURNEY so that you may PROGRESS AS QUICKLY AS POSSIBLE AND AS THOR-OUGHLY AS POSSIBLE TOWARDS YOUR GOAL. Your goal is SPIRITUAL GROWTH - a goal which spreads over MANY AGES and which involves MANY DIFFERENT ENCOUNTERS, often with the same group of souls assisting each other.

YOUR CHILD IS SUCH A PERSON, EVER CONNECTED TO YOU IN SERVICE, AND EVER GRATEFUL FOR SERVICES YOU HAVE RENDERED AND WHICH YOU WILL CONTINUE TO RENDER IN THE FUTURE. You will hold hands again and dance through eternity in various roles, cementing your relationship with each experience and with each incarnation.

QUESTION ABOUT THE SOUL ENTERING THE FOETUS

Speaking of unborn babies and souls, Seraphin, I have often wondered when and how the soul enters the foetus?
Would you elaborate on this?

ANSWER FROM SERAPHIN

Greetings to you. It seems like a deep mystery, does it not, that life should enter a small and helpless body. And yet this is a process closely overseen by specialists and advisors, and one which is best left to them. This is not my speciality.

Although it is beyond the realms of your imagination and beyond the realms of the vocabulary presently at your disposal, know that this happens at exactly the right time for everyone, in alignment with their mandate and the circumstances they have chosen to "surround" and enable their next experience. The timing varies according to individual progress and needs.

In addition, we would like to say that the word "soul" is used in many different ways and also MISUSED, resulting in great confusion. We assume that you mean the lighting of the life spark as in the MIND in a body which so far is limited purely to the physical. The process of actually receiving a GOD SPARK is initiated by the first moral choice - the first show of conscience - shown by the individual concerned. The full expansion of our saturation with divine spirit is achieved through the continual raising of vibration through loving behaviour and dealing with karmic issues and clearing the path for divine connections to be made. This is a rough description of what your development - if you choose the learning journey - may look like.

QUESTION ABOUT BIRTH

I do often wonder about birth, Seraphin. I was a premature baby, whereas my siblings were born two weeks after their "due date". Is there a spiritual or genetic reason for this? While we have the technology now to preserve the life of premature babies, this was not the case in the past and many died.

ANSWER FROM SERAPHIN

Greetings to you. Ponder the fact that your "premature" birth was not actually so, but that as a soul you may have been "mature" enough to surface. Nothing happens by chance, but by divine will and synchronicity. Many premature children have sharp minds and deep spiritual affinities. They wish to "enter the fray", so to speak, and enter the spiritual arena although their bodies might not be able to deal with the physicality of the situation to an optimal degree. But this does not stop them. If a child wishes to make an appearance, it will do so and use any opportunity given to it. The position of the mother on this - whether conscious or subconscious - is also involved.

The development of technology has enabled these souls desiring to enter life outside the womb before the "normal" time, to survive as the result of such a choice. The quality of the "genetic" physical material will also have a bearing on this matter. Those who are more content to take things slowly, or to "drag their feet" a little, or to stay in their cosy comfort zone (in this case, the womb of the mother) may continue to do so in their physical life, though progress can always be initiated by the soul concerned.

QUESTION ABOUT OUR HIGHER SELF

Seraphin: what exactly is my higher self? I have heard the term "higher self" many times, but I'm not exactly sure what it means. Would you explain what my higher self is and also my relationship to my higher self? Perhaps, if I understood this relationship better I would be able to communicate a little better.

ANSWER FROM SERAPHIN

Greetings to you: some of this has been addressed in a previous question, but we would like to add that the term used (Higher Self and similar) is less important in itself, and more important as a divine aspect of yourself which it is everyone's task to try and INTEGRATE into your daily living so that you are ONE, so that your intuition is always finely tuned, as opposed to only in certain reflective or intuitive moments. This means that each step you take - whether physical or mental, will be in a frame of mind which involves care, love, self-confidence and integrity. Above all, watchfulness and mindfulness (a quality often advocated by the Buddhist path) is a quality which abounds in this state of being. An intense awareness of DIVINE SYNCHRONICITY is another. This does not mean that you dwell on every small event, watching in fear for something which indicates that something foreboding is going to happen, but moving forward with EYES OPEN and noticing anything which suddenly jumps out at you as being significant. Even if the meaning of this does not strike you immediately, you may find out later as you embody more and more of your "higher self" into your lower self, as you are more and more connected, as you are more and more aligned with the directives and intentions and purpose of the higher self which is guided by the highest motives and principles.

Regarding communication; imagine that you have a best friend who is always considerate, always offers good advice, who is always compassionate and who is ALWAYS THERE FOR YOU, WHATEVER TIME OF THE DAY OR NIGHT. When you have issues to solve, just talk to this "higher" part of yourself as you would talk to this friend. The more you do this, the deeper your trust in this friend will develop. This is what is meant by DEVELOPING THE INNER CONNECTION, or hearing the INNER VOICE. As we already said, the designation is not so important. It is YOUR STRIVING TO CONNECT TO IT WHICH SHOULD BE THE FOCUS, especially advised for these times.

QUESTION ABOUT ACCESSING DIVINE KNOWLEDGE

Seraphin: I have often heard that the way to progress is "going within"; but have not had much success with that. For a long time, I was disheartened by the continual urging to "go within", knowing it was pointless unless I actually received answers. At the mere suggestion of "going within", my reaction became one of rejection, knowing I wouldn't receive answers, thus considering it pointless. I still have this attitude to a great degree, which is not a happy state of affairs. However, I have received one mental image of a concrete dam, which is very memorable. I couldn't see the whole dam, but sensed it was immense, as was the body of water behind it. The water created tremendous pressure. The spillways and sluices were dry, save for a few small puddles. Aside from the implied pressure, the scene was peaceful. In this scene, the water represented knowledge. My knowledge. This image made a great deal of sense to me and portrays the frustration I have with meditation and "going within.

What would you advise?

ANSWER FROM SERAPHIN

Greetings to you, and know of your great potential which is still "contained" behind the wall but which – should you allow it to flow – will expand hugely and IN FULL SIGHT. The "dam" symbolises your thought constructs, your imaginings of how things should be, your tendency to follow what others offer as advice, your tendency to keep in the background and puzzle things out yourself, rather than tear the walls down regardless of what others think.

Be aware of your thought processes: if you harbour the conviction that you "know you will not receive", then that is what will manifest. If there is fear about what might or might not be revealed, you will not want to accept the truth even if it raises its head. If you approach mediation in a formal way, then you may expect formal, comprehensive or perfect or conventional replies, according to your perception. But this would mean that YOUR PARTICIPATION IS NOT INCLUDED. YOU MUST MAKE THE ASSOCIATION AND INTERPRET WHAT IS SHOWN TO YOU.

In your case, it may be best to delete the word "meditation" from your vocabulary as there are so many associations connected with it. Try to see the whole thing in a completely causal and unorganised manner. It is like walking down a street and suddenly walking up to a front door of a house and ringing the bell because you suspect that your friend might be at home, and you have something in your heart which you would like to discuss. The only difference is that – in the scenario of connecting to the DIVINE – THERE IS ALWAYS SOMEONE AT HOME. THE DOOR WILL ALWAYS OPEN. AND THE FRIEND INSIDE WILL ALWAYS HAVE THE RIGHT ANSWER FOR YOU. It is that simple.

Your world is so OVERLOADED with all sort of layers of disinformation and also attempts to make money (yes, the MEDITATION SCENE, where learning this costs money, is also part of that), and it is necessary to CLEAR all these vestiges from your mind completely. This is a PERSONAL CONNECTION and there are no rules. It is a connection which YOU YOURSELF CREATE, just as you create everything else which happens in your life. If it works for you, you can imagine that a PINK ELEPHANT OPENS THAT DOOR and that he speaks to you in a language you do not understand, and that you then draw your own conclusions from the TONE of his answers. You can imagine that this is a door of a large castle and that it takes HOURS to find the throne room where the King will provide the answers to your questions, but you might find that IN THE COURSE OF WALKING LOST DOWN THE CORRIDORS, answers or ideas may come. You may imagine going through that door and instantly falling into a very deep hole so that you spend all that time falling wondering when the crash will be and what you will land on, and in the intensity of those moments, the saving truth may come to you.

Do you see where I am going with this?

I repeat that THERE ARE NO RULES, AND NO CERTAIN TIME TO DO THIS, AND NO NEED FOR LONG HOURS OF SITTING AND "TRYING" to meditate.

Apart from visualisations like the ones I have just mentioned, pay attention in your waking state which can turn into a continuous "meditative" state of PAYING ATTENTION TO ONE'S STEPS from a rather objective point of view, seeing oneself as a stranger going down certain paths and reflecting on that. If you once received a certain "message" not to participate in group meditations, it is because that was very structured. THIS WOULD HAVE

BEEN NO GOOD FOR YOU, BECAUSE YOU HAD ALREADY DEVELOPED YOUR OWN STRUCTURES AND IDEAS AND WOULD NOT WELL FIT INTO THIS PARTICULAR COURSE OF INSTRUCTION AT THAT TIME.

While it may have helped others, in ways that they themselves decided, this was not for you at this time. You are a strong individual and must follow your own path with determination.

You mention being at a loss of how to proceed. We advise you not to think about the HOW and just to plunge into LIFE IN ALL ITS FULLNESS. Do not hold anything back. Do not be the DAM which holds back your vitality. This applies to all areas of life. To live in FULLNESS is to be an EXAMPLE to others around you, to act as a CATALYST for the journey of others. And it will also move you from a place of hesitation and worry to a place of confidence and GREAT JOY. We thank you for bringing up your personal story, as we know it will help others here on their path.

QUESTION ON DIVINE INTUITION

Dear Seraphin: is there any value in distinguishing the differences in where my intuition, gut feeling or inner dialogue is coming from? Just the fact that there is inner guidance available seems to be a great blessing to begin with.

But is it only a stepping stone to greater communications from within? Are there qualities in this process that distinguishes whom we're getting our inspiration from, for example our higher self or guardian? Or does it even matter as long as we are open to listening from within?

ANSWER FROM SERAPHIN

Greetings. We recognise the great attraction of delving into the world of philosophical thought. For several, it is a valid form of retreat and contemplation which enables deep insight and fascinating new perspectives. If, however, there is a great deal of time spent attempting to distinguish minor variances - you might call it "splitting hairs" - then this is a waste of precious energy more suitably directed elsewhere. This is not a personal comment or judgement, but rather it applies generally across the board as something which SLOWS PROCESSES DOWN RATHER THAN SPEEDING THEM UP. So, in answer to your question; there is much discussion in different forums/organisations/religions regarding the correct term for that part of ourselves which is the TRUE CORE, THE AUTHENTIC CORE, THE DIVINE FRAGMENT, THE MIRROR OF ALL, THE ONE, THE TRUTH. It is a great blessing, as you say, to recognise THAT IT EXISTS AND THAT IT CAN PROVIDE US WITH ANSWERS. It is not a great blessing to spend much deliberation on how to call it. Much confusion exists on this world, and as such you are to be commended for your question. In the future, when all are united in one language, certain definitions will be decided upon in order to form a clear and cohesive picture. Concerning qualities in the process: everyone who embarks on this inner journey will discover this step by step. One of the "landmarks" of the journey is noticing that there is a sort of physical feeling which accompanies your inner thought and communion sessions. For this scribe, it feels like a waterfall of energy falling upon her at some junctures when she connects. For others, it may be something completely different. Each according to their own perception and their own journey. And to conclude: yes, your openness will always allow for forward propulsion.

QUESTION ON SOULMATES

Seraphin, could you tell us more about soulmates?

ANSWER FROM SERAPHIN

Greetings to you. Indeed, I can talk about "soulmates", but perhaps not in the fashion you might expect. The perverted view of "love" on this planet has led to many a romantic illusion and many a deep disappointment. The seed has been sewn - by those who seek to destroy adherence to the Laws of Balance and Creation - so that the search for a soulmate is uppermost and so that your finding of such will be the fulfilment of your existence here, to live "happily ever after" so to speak. Thus you are encouraged to desert your true path for this "love".

However, the definition of a soulmate is:

SOMEONE WHO WITNESSES YOU AND YOUR POTENTIAL AND STRIVES TO PROMOTE NOT ONLY YOUR HAPPINESS BUT ALSO YOUR VERY UNIQUE AND INDIVIDUAL SERVICE TO THE ONE.

And this person will not miraculously appear in front of you. This person will be ATTRACTED TO YOUR PATH, IF YOUR PATH IS STRONG ENOUGH AND ATTRACTIVE ENOUGH.

It is not YOU but your ACTIONS AND INTENT which will find another person WALKING THE SAME ROAD WITH THE SAME HONOURABLE INTENTIONS. This is the ideal relationship: enjoying MUTUAL SUPPORT IN ORDER TO REACH WORTHY GOALS. Thus, to "find" your soulmate / partner / spiritual friend, define and follow your aims as precisely as possible. Thus will you share the same journey and be perfectly matched.

QUESTION ON THE MISUSE OF THE WORD CHRIST

With so much done in Christ's name which is against life, Seraphin, I wonder will there be a direct address to or exposure of the people who have used this name to attain powerful positions? Will there be a way to analyse history- perhaps in the Akashic Records - and to address how Christ concepts were successfully articulated as well as manipulated by historical Christian figures? I am wondering what sort of justice will be served on behalf of Christ's name.

ANSWER FROM SERAPHIN

Greetings to you, and thank you for bringing in the historical perspective which has indeed been much warped by those you call "historians".

What has been officially recorded is only a partial truth related from a partial perspective. And there will be full disclosure of this so that the absurdity of making war in the name of GOD, where both sides were absolutely convinced of their own right, will be fully disclosed.

As those leaders recognised, there was great power to be gained - great manipulative power in fact - to say GOD IS ON OUR SIDE. In another sense; GOD IS ALWAYS ON YOUR SIDE, in the sense that your angels and guardians do continually attempt - within their mandate and preserving your free will simultaneously - to direct you towards your fulfilment and vocation. Due to teachings and concepts which will completely revolutionise your ideas of what GOD is and does, it will soon become obvious that in such episodes of your history, much has been distorted.

It will also become obvious that many were deceived or let themselves be deceived. Technology providing insights into the Akashic records will be available in the future, and then even more will become clear.

Furthermore, the idea that someone is RIGHT and another person is WRONG will fade into the background, as such judging processes are not the focus of a spiritual society. The focus is on constant DEVELOPMENT, and all stages will inevitably contribute to this forward development.

In addition, seeing something as "Christ-embracing" or Christ-rejecting" will not be seen in a religious context. To carry Christ awareness is to behave like a Christed being, but as there are many belief systems and also many old masters returning, WHO WERE ALSO CHRISTED BEINGS, suitable terminology will be found by them to describe this desired state of consciousness.

Such are some of the new ways you will see your old world.

QUESTION ABOUT LOW-LEVEL CONSCIOUSNESS

Seraphin: my question is regarding the low level in consciousness in the so called 3rd world countries. It is well known that in these countries the level of education is very low, which often leads to vandalism, corruption, drugs abuse, etc.

Can minds of low consciousness be restructured to adapt to the higher vibrations which will be on earth in the future, or will they not be able to stay due to an inability to adapt?

ANSWER FROM SERAPHIN

Greetings to you. We see that you are very concerned about countries who are seen to be less advantaged than others. Comparisons can of course be made, but may also be misleading if taken in a very broad context such as this.

The definition of what true "education" is, is another point for discussion. Many people in your so-called "advanced" countries have been stuffed with a great deal of superfluous and erroneous knowledge, and this says very little about their actual level of consciousness which is actually the yardstick for remaining on this earth. Similarly, there may be many people in so-called "third world countries" who have a deeper understanding of what is really going on here, who are close to the ground as in having a close affinity to nature, and whose level of wisdom is considerable. Imagine a beekeeper in a mountain meadow who knows little about academic study. He will know, however, from his dealing with the bees, that there is something in the air infecting nature which destroys natural cycles and affects his very livelihood.

"Vandalism, corruption and drugs" is not something related to third world countries only. It is rampant in so-called advanced countries such as the United States. "Lower-consciousness minds" can always improve. This is not a case of someone "restructuring" from outside, but simply a personal decision and desire to learn. If this is not possible - to make this switch to a line of enquiry - then such souls will be placed in another environment which is suitable for their present pace of learning, even if that pace is almost stationary. This is the humane way to deal with this situation, and the teams dealing with this have a great deal of experience.

QUESTION ABOUT FREE WILL

How can we "wake people up" spiritually without interfering with their free-will, Seraphin? It is quite easy if loved ones ask questions, because then they are open to a response and legitimate answer. Most of the time though there is silence when I share some information and I worry if I am crossing a "free-will" boundary that is going to reap negative karma back to me.

My heart is sincere in wanting everyone I love to "know" about all the lies and deceit and yet I know that we should not interfere with their free-will.

ANSWER FROM SERAPHIN

Greetings to you. We applaud your concern for your family. Please remember that IF you decide to share information, it is your decision and free will to do so, and it is the free will and decision of your relatives to decide whether to respond, say nothing, be inquisitive but not dare to ask immediately because they don't want to sound stupid, or any other scenario or reason you can imagine.

It is very difficult to assess in advance the responses of others, often because you may have a certain "fixed" idea of them and their capabilities for comprehension. However, you and also your friends and relations ARE ALWAYS CHANGING, so this means that the your anticipation of them not responding may be erroneous. This is where personal initiative jumps in. Every situation is a new one, and it is imperative that you try and leave old ideas about others out of the scenario. If you are convinced in advance that no-one will listen to you, then that is exactly what will happen, as your fear of this and of rejection will reduce your words to a certain framework. Please try and let that go.

Anything, including very interesting and wondrous develop-ments, are possible when someone has an open mind and when the point from which one ventures is a STATE OF AUTHENTIC-ITY WHERE YOU ARE EXPRESSING YOUR DEEP AND HEARTFELT FEELINGS AND YOUR DEEP CONCERN FOR OTHERS. If others FEEL that you are coming from a place of REALLY DEEP CONCERN FOR THEM, they will recognise this despite the somewhat "strange" information you are passing on to them.

Whether to speak or not is your own decision. Whether you do so or not is not a case of right or wrong. It is not a case of an opportunity missed or taken, for all information reaches the right ears at the right time. There are situations where someone is just not ready to absorb information, even if clearly put and relevant. Or someone unexpected may burst in while you are talking. This will disrupt and will also be a sign that your audience is not ready. It has no bearing on the truth you are speaking. We hope that this may serve as an orientation for your behaviour.

QUESTION ABOUT THE HEALING POWER OF LOVE

Does love heal, Seraphin?
Can the body self-heal by holding a high vibration of love?

ANSWER FROM SERAPHIN

My greetings to you. The love vibration is indeed a healing vibra-tion, and if you are a vessel holding this vibration, it will affect you (and whoever encounters you) in a positive way, should others be open and receptive to it. This can also be part of daily practice: you can monitor your thoughts carefully and discover which of them are NOT IN ALIGNMENT WITH THE LOVE VIBRATION.

This, as always, does not mean that you should stop standing your ground if you see people who are violating certain important principles, but that you should be aware of the general state of your mind and its fluctuations. If the fluctuations are very high, then simply watch this. The very act of watching will reduce the fluctuations.

This is an area in which there will be assistance in the future, in the form of teaching, but it can be started NOW, and at any time. A mere smile can cause WAVES OF LOVE TO TRAVEL FAR. And it can connect you to people who you may have considered GLUM AND UNAPPROACHABLE. Be astounded at their responses. Know that there is always more to discover about oneself and others. Try to bridge the gap.

QUESTION ABOUT SPORTS

Dear Seraphin. I have been working and dealing with sports for many years, and I have always felt that sports are something good which bring people to a healthier life-style and closer to nature. But at the same time (like with almost everything on this planet), we created many unholy aspects like lots of competition that create separation, or ego influenced motivation to beat the others. I guess you can see where my question goes. I have been trying to create a better idea of a more spiritual connection to sports that should be developed on this planet. So, your insights and perspective about it would be very welcome!

Maybe these will be called "physical recreational activities that connect mind and body", and maybe they already exist on more spiritually advanced planets.

ANSWER FROM SERAPHIN

Greetings to you, the WANDERER AND DISCOVERER. By your own example and experience, you have indeed DISCOVERED that movement brings new awareness and insights, and thus we delight in your question concerning sport, and we delight in answering it thus, as the next Seraphin Message. We applaud your constant desire to acquire more information and to move swiftly along the spiritual path. May all those who read here take the following passage to heart.

Seraphin Message 238: THE SPIRITUALITY OF SPORT
Through Rosie, 26th August 2015

"Sport", in your present understanding on planet earth, is a variation of peripheral practice to be undertaken in one's free time in order to improve one's health. This is the sort of general statement which does little to cover this very vast area which is not confined to the physical realm. The secondary (or for some, the primary) purpose of sport is to provide entertainment for the masses, serving as a distraction from areas of consideration which actually NEED YOUR ATTENTION DESPERATELY.

Here we are talking about the phenomenon rife in Roman times also where the populace was subdued by BREAD AND GAMES. Let these spectacles not deter you, inhabitants of earth, from that which is of true importance. Do not reduce yourselves to lethargic onlookers who move and live vicariously through others, ignoring critical issues. We would like to draw your attention to the following important learning opportunities provided by practising physical exercise.

BALANCE

To practice balancing exercises is to identify the degree of your centeredness and the degree to which you easily lose control over your intentions. How determined are you, and how carefully do you proceed towards your goal? You can simulate this by walking along a fallen tree trunk, holding the question in your mind. As within, so without. This will give you some indication of your present state of mind and whether you need to slow down or speed up to keep an even keel.

ALACRITY OF RESPONSE

There are various martial arts practised on your earth with the intent of training alacrity of response and overcoming opposition. To train in this way will have an undoubted effect on your THINK-ING PROCESSES which will become more fine-tuned as a result. Co-creative momentum is another aspect of such practices; the energy "given" by your "opponent/co-creator can be used to rebound/regive an even greater energy. A synergy effect or joint propulsion effect is achieved.

This is also reflected on a spiritual level in the sense of WHEN TWO PEOPLE MEET IN THE NAME OF DIVINITY. Especially in the coming period of great distress, but also of great opportunity, you who read here will be presented with many chances to test your alacrity of response.

TRUST IN ONESELF AND IN ONE'S OWN POWER is another side effect of these arts. To increase one's self esteem is important in a world which seeks to keep you – using many methods psychological and manipulative – in mental shackles.

TEAMWORK AND COOPERATION

Team games, if not used to incite hatred or the feeling that one side is "better" or "faster" or "worth more" than the other – can improve cooperation skills and also encourage different team members (who may not feel such an affinity to each other) to work together to achieve a common aim. Many teams of different sorts will soon be active in the many areas on your planet which require transformation, renovation and improvement.

There will be much to rebuild and re-invent.

As individuals, you will not be capable of this. As teams whose members constantly look out for one another and who focus on a certain task, this will run optimally. This can be practised in team sports, and working in teams will become an essential part of schooling in the future.

DISCIPLINE AND CONCENTRATION

Whatever the genre of sport, to practice it is to increase one's concentration and focus. This may be especially exemplified, for example, by control of a sword in various martial arts, or in the degree of accuracy required to shoot an arrow so that it hits the bull's eye.

This is a metaphor for your STRIVING FOR PERFECTION, for straining to be as effective as possible by developing the talents which you possess. If this process takes place on a physical level through archery or similar, this will influence your focus in non-physical processes.

TAKING CARE OF THE PHYSICAL TEMPLE

One great benefit of sporting activities – and here we include all forms of movement fast or slow – is the enhancement of the physical temple, your body which – similar to your cars, bicycles or airplanes – requires checking and overhauling and cleaning and checking of internal engines and cogs so that EVERYTHING FUNCTIONS PERFECTLY. Through physical movement you can be made aware of blockages in your body system, which in turn are symptoms of psychological blockages. Thus, training your body is not just a way to spend free time or a way to impress others through your physical stature or "fitness", but an instrument of physical and mental cleansing.

MOVING THROUGH NATURE
AND CONTACT WITH THE ELEMENTS

As many sports take place out of doors, this puts you in direct contact with the elements, especially the element of earth and air. You develop a more refined consciousness of the hardness or softness of the earth beneath your feet, and you increase your awareness of the air passing through your mouth and nostrils as a result of increased intake or being – from time to time – temporarily "OUT OF BREATH. This is a quickening of all systems to see how you cope under stress, yet you can always stop if necessary and you can always lie down on your ever-loving and supporting earth if that is your requirement.

Thus, you learn to pace yourself, and your close contact with nature itself and viewing her processes teaches you how to PACE YOURSELF ACCORDINGLY AND IN ALIGNMENT.

EVERY MOVE IS A HOLY MOVE

This your aim: to make every move a holy move, not by putting pressure upon yourself as in NOW I HAVE TO DO SPORT FOR ONE HOUR or NOW I HAVE TO MEDITATE FOR ONE HOUR BECAUSE PEOPLE SAY IT IS GOOD FOR ME. A meditative state can be as simple as running in the forest in a relaxed but yet attentive way. A meditative state can also be as simple as swimming slowly in a lake, savouring every second. It is in moments such as these that you can not only relax but also be privy to MOMENTS OF INTENSE INSPIRATION which serve to assist your present situations. The physical movement supports your immediate sense of being completely IN THE NOW, unencumbered by tortuous thoughts of who said what, of the week's agenda, of what people or yourself expect of you. Removing yourself from the daily routine to experience physical movement can bring about such moments of great insight.

EXERCISING PHYSICAL MUSCLES AND
SPIRITUAL MUSCLES

In short, the benefit of exercising your physical muscles is parallel to exercising your spiritual muscles, and they complement and further one another. Your physical body contains and stores ALL INFORMATION ABOUT ALL EXPERIENCES IN YOUR LIFE SO FAR, and so any physical signs your body may be giving you WILL RELATE TO THIS. Use your physical experiences to move ever inward on the road to self-knowledge, and this will surely stand you in good stead concerning your physical health and also your mental prowess which will enable you to react to outward situations in a calm, appropriate and measured response.

QUESTION ON SEEING THE SAME NUMBER REPEATEDLY

Dear Seraphin: can you please explain repetitive numbers? Why does it happen? Who is prompting us to see them? What does it mean - if anything? Should we be doing something when this occurs? Are we attracting repetitive numbers to ourselves? I feel that I never get a clear explanation. I read that when you see repetitive numbers – it is angels or guides who are trying to get your attention. I used to see 11:11 for a long time. Then it changed to 144, which has been consistent over the past few years. I see 144 everywhere - even following a car with the license plate 144. I'm sure I know what it means (I smile to myself and say thank you) but I think it would be beneficial to have an explanation because many people ask me about repetitive numbers or bring it to my attention. Maybe it's all airy fairy New Age stuff - then maybe not.

ANSWER FROM SERAPHIN

Greetings to you. We recognise your gifting to others. Concerning numbers, or any other repetitive signs or incidents or words or symbols or "coincidences", know that all these are ways used by your guides or angels for GAINING YOUR ATTENTION. This gaining of attention, however, is not just to recognise that something is cumulating or occurring often, but recognising that there is a NEED TO GO INTO ACTION IN SOME WAY. To simply see that numbers are recurring and to assume that this is just a way that someone is trying to say "hello" is erroneous. There is a purpose behind this. If such coincidences have little meaning for those observing them, we recommend going into quiet meditation and ASKING WHY this is happening, or what action should be taken when the sign appears again.

We can give you a good example of this. This scribe noticed that her fourth finger on one hand itched again and again at certain intervals. At first, she thought it was some sort of a physical ailment or irritation which would not go away. It recurred and recurred again. When she ASKED she received the answer that this was a sign that something needed to be CREATED by her. Later she came into the realisation that I WAS ASKING HER TO CREATE A MESSAGE TOGETHER WITH ME.

Indeed, there is a very serious possibility of being submerged by "new age fluffy stuff". We advise always getting down to practicalities and setting about problems in a concrete way following internal consultation.

QUESTION ABOUT KARMA

Dear Seraphin: if one is truly sorry about transgressions/hurts committed against others in the past, is karma eradicated
or softened a bit?

ANSWER FROM SERAPHIN

Greetings to you. You have a GREAT INNER EYE. We say this as we see the sort of work you are doing, and the great potential which you have to increase this in ways you have not thought yet possible. This, in fact, is a valid statement for all who read here.

Being truly sorry for transgressions means never even entertaining repeating such. This means taking a completely different new direction, never again relapsing into old damaging habits or tendencies. This represents A LESSON LEARNT. If a lesson is learnt in its entirety in this way, then indeed the vibrations one sends out are completely different, and the result of such higher vibratory level will have the effect of producing positive experiences and positive repercussions. If one is truly and genuinely sorry for a short while, that will have a short-lived effect, but if this is continuous, you will be blessed by what you send out in the sense of WHAT YOU GIVE, YOU WILL RECEIVE. If suddenly faced with "karma" nevertheless, this is the result of a different seed you have sewn BUT NOT REALISED AT THE TIME.

So does your learning journey continue, and so does your perception of what optimal behaviour actually consists in continue. You are in fact ever refining your perception, ever increasing the quality of your behaviour as a result of scrutinising what events and incidents cross your path, ESPECIALLY THOSE YOU DO NOT WISH TO SEE IN YOUR PATH. This is the long journey to perfection and to Paradise.

QUESTION ABOUT BELL TONES

Of late, Seraphin, I have been woken up by a certain sound – sometimes it is a chime, and sometimes it is a bell. Is this a test? Is this a sign that I am "downloading" information telepathically? Does this have something to do with my mission?

ANSWER FROM SERAPHIN

Greetings to you.
It has often been said that bells issue warnings,
or that they intend to "wake-up",
or that they are used to "call people together",
or any other interpretation you can think of.
And this is in fact the main issue here;
YOUR INTERPRETATION.

You can of course ask me or anyone else if they have experienced bells, and each will have their own answer, and each answer will be valid from their perception, but their answers may or may not resonate with you.

So, in this case, it is your task to track when these bells occur and immediately ask your inner self WHAT THEY MEAN. This you may write down, so as to fix it in your memory. And whenever the bells occur, you may write down your feelings connected with them. Because nothing happens by chance, the occurrence of the bells will not happen by chance either.

Please remember that the bells themselves are of not so significant. The significance is the LEARNING WHICH THEY CAN BRING. This does not have to do with telepathy. Telepathy is mind to mind communication, just as I am communicating my thoughts to the mind of this scribe at this very moment. Whether the bell is associated in any way with new information is again a case for your own investigation.

Regarding your mission and in fact generally, as far as missions are concerned: all would do well to look at their lives so far and assess their position and pinpoint the times when you really felt you were contributing to something important in a really useful way, not in a way which expands ego or increases the income, but one which serves humanity.

You are ALREADY LIVING YOUR MISSION, and have already lived your mission, whether you have done this in a high-profile way or in a low-profile way, whether you have put a lot of energy into it or just a little. IDENTIFY YOUR MISSION SO FAR AND CONTINUE IT. If you have stopped, START WHERE YOU LEFT

OFF. Do not continually look to the future, for your future missions WILL BE BASED ON WHAT YOU ACHIEVED IN THE PAST, AND HOW YOU ARE APPROACHING THINGS NOW. We wish you all great investigations into determining what you have done well, and what line of action you wish to continue.

QUESTION ON THE SIGNIFICANCE OF DREAMS

Dear Seraphin. Last night I dreamt of a little blonde girl traveling to the west USA in a covered wagon and we were attacked by Native Americans. I was scalped and died as a little girl - thus I lost my blonde hair - along with my life. In this life, ever since I was a small, I felt that I should be blonde and I dye my hair to be so. Do past life dreams also serve up lessons?

ANSWER FROM SERAPHIN

Greetings to you. You can rest assured that any vivid dreams will have some meaning for you, and that it is for YOURSELF to interpret exactly what there is to be learned from that. Association is also of prominence here. If other dreams are looked at IN COMBINATION with this one from the times of the "wild west", there will be more to discover.

Treating experiences in isolation is one of the greatest diseases on this planet, as is regarding oneself as isolated from the rest of humanity and indeed from the rest of the universe. As you can see, I am opening up huge vistas for you here, as regards space, and I can open up more huge vistas for you if I suggest all the other lives you have experienced where you were not blond and not female.

So, the question remains: why is this a "burning question" for you at this particular point in time? Perhaps your attention could shift to the other qualities of the young girl, rather than the physical qualities (the hair). To be youthful is often to be SPONTANEOUS AND FULL OF LIFE AND ENERGY. In later years, for many reasons, this SAP OF LIFE may tend to fall away. The invitation is to pursue WHAT is promoting this, and how can one retain one's vitality instead of being dragged down.

We recommend making lists of activities - to be periodically pursued - which uplift your spirits and make you feel LIKE A YOUNG GIRL WITH BLONDE HAIR. The physical attribute is rarely significant. The quality of VITALITY is.

QUESTION ABOUT OUR MISSIONS

I am a Reiki healing practitioner. Yet, for the last 9 years I have been working in industry as a computer programmer analyst. How does this tie in with my healing training?

ANSWER FROM SERAPHIN

Greetings to you of the SEVERAL DIFFERENT PROFESSIONS WHICH SHALL MERGE AS ONE. In time, you will see that all threads you have been following will join as one. Your expertise in the realm of industry will serve you well as this is an important area, especially when it comes to closing down such operations and implementing new ones. As you are aware, the closure of mammoth projects can cause a great deal of emotional distress which is the result of not wishing to release something which has been considered essential as a service, or which represents a milestone in one's path. Thus will you encounter many people who require spiritual help of all kinds, and you will be in a position to offer assistance on all fronts. There is no separation in the various avenues which may be pursued during a certain lifetime; they run parallel in the sense that they serve the promotion of each other, even if one leaves one path for good. Such an action then propels you towards something which you perceive as being "better" or more worthy. But without the hindsight and previous experience, the present path would not be possible.

This is how you are to view your lives so far - as contributing to THE MOMENT NOW. All is valuable. Nothing is lost or "wasted time", and everything is part of the learning journey. We are excited to see how you will personally apply your experience and knowledge in the opportunities which will arise for you.

SERAPHIN ANSWERS QUESTIONS ON THE UNSEEN

QUESTIONS ABOUT ANGELIC BEINGS

Here are some questions for you dear Seraphin:
Do angelic beings ever sleep or rest?
What about the other Celestials?
Are some more physical than others?
What about nourishment?
Do celestials become couples?

ANSWER FROM SERAPHIN

Greetings to you of the INQUISITIVE MIND. As my scribe has already stated recently, CURIOSITY is very much to be welcomed, especially when it comes to INVESTIGATING YOURSELVES and your reactions. This is the time of great revelations, but how can you reveal to yourselves your true glory when you are still turning your gaze in a direction which is outside of yourselves? We leave this question with you to contemplate further.

Do we of the angelic realms rest?

The need to rest arises – quite logically - when there is a need to pause, to clear, to contemplate, to reflect upon what has happened because there is something more to discover. This means that the more clarity you have, the more piercing your gaze, the more you UNDERSTAND FULLY what is going on around you, including the motivations and effects of yourselves and your fellow humans, the less strenuous will your lives become, and the less rest will be needed. This is a very general and broad-brush statement, yet you may be able to interpret it for yourselves. When you feel overwhelmed or not able to cope with something difficult or - in your view – unsolvable – many of you will choose to retreat, to not engage, to wallow in emotion. Some people will even to go to bed and shut everything out.

Sleep will allow you to have a rest – a space where a degree of objectivity can be introduced, a space where complications may be able to start unravelling, a place where options and solutions and alternative perspectives may be presented to the mind which is open.

In addition to this, sleep is necessary for those who OVERLOAD their bodies with food in great quantities and with poison. Much of your food is presently contaminated, as are your soils and air. This low level of quality will have its effect on the human material which is your body. These physical factors combined with the emotional and mental and psychological factors, make sleep necessary.

Those who are in complete balance and continually connected to the Divine in the sense of constant knowledge of their own divinity and potential to manifest their path in accordance with the laws which govern the universe – these highly "spiritual" beings have no need of a break or of sleep, simply because EVERYTHING IS CONTINUALLY BEING DIGESTED AND WORKED UPON IN IDEAL BALANCE, MOTION AND FLOW so that there is NO BACKLOG TO ADDRESS.

Contemplate that you are always dragging this "backlog" behind you and that this slows you down. Sleep replenishes you and provides you with new strength.

Concerning nourishment, according to your level of spiritual development, different foods are appropriate. Those who can digest all completely do not produce waste products, for example.

Those who are active mainly in a mental and not a physical realm will not require "physical food" in the sense that you understand it. Again, this is very general. Your universe is populated with so many different sorts of beings of diverse origins that it would be impossible to give a quick overview here.

Regarding whether celestials form couples; there are indeed pairs of beings whose "relationships" are very, very longstanding and who together accomplish great things even if they are not constantly together as you would view it in the traditional sense.

This is possible due to constant contact which you might term "telepathic". Their "babies" are not always physically real; they can be plans conceived by both which then reach fruition.

With higher beings, these plans are always for the good of others and have nothing to do with "cementing a relationship". Their focus is on the universal family, which they serve, rather than the small family unit. Yet this is not a general rule.

Again, there are so many different beings in this universe, all at different stages of development using different bodies for their various tasks.

The solutions to their concerns are – let us say – drawn from a pool of potential to which you on earth are not yet privy.

As always, I am trying here to convey that the perimeters of your understanding and imagination are just that – PERIMETERS – and that there are so many more scenarios and possibilities than you can at present conceive of.

QUESTION ABOUT OUT OF BODY TRAVEL

Seraphin: how can we achieve astral travel and conscious out of body experiences?

ANSWER FROM SERAPHIN

Greetings to you whose enthusiasm is worthy, yet the question is less one of HOW CAN I ACHIEVE THESE ABILITIES and more a question of WHAT IS MY INTENTION.

Many see such abilities as a sort of magic which will release them from the mundane aspects and profanities of life, yet they themselves have chosen and created this life and it is their challenge to address the complexities and labyrinths of what they have personally put in place. Learning extraordinary abilities will not iron out the problems in their lives. Indeed, it is the other way around. Addressing personal issues, which translate into negative situations in the physical realm, will raise their vibrations and consciousness so that their progress to the next stage – whatever hill they wish to climb – will be effortless. This will be part of a natural order instead of a sudden leap into the "supernatural". It will be a stairway of many small steps instead of an enormous leap.

We suggest the patient, humble and ever-striving way towards an increase in self-awareness. Watch yourselves. Watch every breath and every word and every reaction from others. Practice constant adjustment. Use every small opportunity to learn more and move a small step forward. Do this not with a sense of fear or with a sense of absolute determination, but with an air of heightened expectation and poise. Never lose your balance on the stairway. Assess yourselves daily. There are many who are out of balance in their daily lives and in their encounters with others. There are those who will bite their lips when they should speak. There are those who will fall into an angry rage at the sight of a certain person or at the sound of a particular word. These are triggers determining your behaviour and we entreat you to STEP OUT of such scenarios and view them objectively, thus favouring your own balance.

This quality of being able to remain in balance will serve you much more in the chaotic times to come than the ability to "escape" on astral travel or similar. Stay in the physical realm. Your sorties into meditation and the inner world are to FIND ASSISTANCE FOR YOUR JOURNEY IN THE PHYSICAL REALM. This is why you are presently stationed on a physical planet in a physical body – to enhance the lives of others THROUGH THE UPLIFTING OF YOURSELVES.

Again I say: all your thoughts and actions TRANSLATE INTO THE PHYSICAL FORM. This is why you see so many examples of imbalance in your societies and encounters. These are the result of the IMBALANCE IN YOUR MINDS AND BEHAVIOUR. The theme of responsibility has been approached and discussed many times. Take this to heart, as only thus will you progress as a global community.

We realise that these words are not all entirely relevant to your original question in that they cover much greater ground than the original enquiry. Yet we use this as a "sounding board" and as an opportunity to teach a greater perspective, for which we thank you deeply.

QUESTION ABOUT DEVIC BEINGS

Dear Seraphin: I would love to know more about devic beings. My limited understanding is that they work with the plant and animal kingdoms, in the growing of food and herbs for medicinal use. I have been humbled by their help in many of my gardening endeavours. I feel great kinship to these beings and want to know how humans can work together with them for the benefit of all? Will they play a role in the future of Earth?

ANSWER FROM SERAPHIN

Greetings to you, dear friend, who has contact to many beings which vastly outnumber those she supposes, and which have a huge variety of names / categories as yet unknown to you in this particular incarnation. It would truly be very difficult for human beings generally to imagine what creatures seen and unseen, what energies seen and unseen, and what growth mechanisms seen and unseen are really in continuous activation on your earth, to say nothing of the influence of incoming energies which presently affect your atmosphere. To call all this "devic" is a vast over-simplification. For experts in this field, this is an even greater simplification. We commend you for your sensitivity for this teeming world which does not usually present itself through current human perceptions. We recommend that you personally to make detailed records of your encounters with these "helpful hands" so that others may start to have this initial peek into a fascinating world of growth and evolution which - as everything else in alignment with the laws of balance - is based on LOVE. Please share your stories for the better understanding between the human world and the plant word. If this is your intent, and you state it to the "devic world", they will surely support your endeavours, provide you with answers and enhance abundance.

QUESTION ON ARGUMENT WITH A DARK ENTITY

Dear Seraphin. I have recently had a "strong thought" or vision in which I was angrily debating with an unseen dark presence, and I do not fully understand what I am supposed to learn from it. Was it important?

ANSWER FROM SERAPHIN

Greetings to you. It seems that you are working towards the light, judging by your experiences. The opening up of awareness can take many forms, including a more refined ability to sense what is really going on, to be more fine-tuned to other people, to be more sensitive to changes in atmosphere, and to notice increasingly the symbolism of what happens around you as being a reflection of what is going on within yourself. If something like the thought you describe suddenly appears, seemingly "out of nowhere", it will in some way be intimately connected with yourself simply because you can PICK UP ON THIS VIBRATION.

If you were arguing with this entity, as suggested, then it involved a very passionate side of yourself which was brought out by this encounter. Often something like this may feel completely unrelated or out of the blue, or it may feel like a voice from the subconscious coming out into the open. This means that it was TIME FOR THE VOICE TO MAKE AN APPEARANCE, AND TIME FOR YOUR EMOTIONS TO SURFACE. This may have been prompted by your personal guides, but this is for you to decide.

We do not address such questions with a simple YES OR NO, since this would detract from your learning experience. Our role here is to AID DISCOVERY, NOT TO PROVIDE ALL THE ANSWERS. We recommend that you go within and ask this entity (or aspect of yourself, should this be the case) to sit opposite you in order to discuss further in a civil manner. Should it be a "negative" experience for you, or should the entity become abusive and get out of the chair, end the session. It is no good "banging your head against a brick wall", trying to convince this entity about something or to argue with it. Insist on a balanced exchange. Then you will be in a position to see whether this is something which will aid your own personal development, or whether it should be continued.

QUESTION ABOUT A POISONOUS PLANT

Dear Seraphin. I have had sudden telepathic communication with a plant known as the common ragwort. It is poisonous and it was growing in the meadow where my horse grazes. The ragwort asked if it was allowed to stay in the field. Although I felt uneasy about it, I recognised that this plant also had a right to be there. I told the plant that it could stay there, but it was not allowed to reproduce. The following year, it was gone. Are poisonous plants really poisonous? Have we assessed them wrongly?

ANSWER FROM SERAPHIN

Greetings to you. Your concern for both the animal world and the plant world and the problems therein have brought you to this point. This is why you were contacted by this plant being – in order to serve as a mediator of sorts.

Your knowledge of horses and what may afflict them has spurred you on to consider everything which is detrimental to their health. It is this investigative approach which is also extremely necessary in the area of human health where this is still sadly lacking, as it is a realm dominated by financial concerns.

Love has little part in this scenario. It is the case on other planets that the plant world and animal world and all other beings are in complete harmony. As she is writing down this answer from me, this scribe has just been bitten by an ant. Even these small occurrences do not occur in the higher vibrations, for each is aware of the potential damage which one could cause to the next.

The plant being which contacted you did so out of a CALL OF CONSCIENCE, with the knowledge that it could – if consumed in large quantities – damage the health of the grazers. Developing a conscience is part of the spiritual journey – an essential part, we may add. It means that you will consider ALL the consequences of your actions, instead of simply regarding the benefit for yourselves.

Consider also that this is a CO-CREATIVE SITUATION and that not only the ragwort but also the horses are involved. If their sensibility is so finely developed that they intuitively KNOW which plant can nurture them, and which plant can harm them, then they would automatically limit their intake and graze selectively.

The parallel on the human level of behaviour on earth can be seen here too. There are many poisons which human beings ingest and which do not kill them (ingestion of the ragwort is poisonous only IN LARGE QUANTITIES) but the potential for causing an end to their life-stream is a given. If the individual decides to overdose, that may be the result. Thus, this is their responsibility and their choice. It is essential, as always to understand that you live in an INTERCONNECTED WORLD, and one in which RESPECT and a certain MODERATION IN CONSUMING AND CONSUMPTION will help to assure overall balance.

QUESTION ON PAST LIVES

Dear Seraphin. As best I can tell, all of us have experienced numerous previous incarnations during which our problematic emotional issues, negative karmic exchanges and patterns, and life path "missions" went unresolved or unfulfilled. I am curious if we are required to reconcile every last bit of karma and negative programming across all lives before advancing. Does the soul select which unresolved issues from past lifetimes it wishes to work through in a life? Does the soul also take on more or less karmic release work depending on whether it intends on clearing undesirable karma and energetic constructs from ancestors or even planets? I'm sure the answers will vary for each unique soul but I am hoping for your general insights on this matter

ANSWER FROM SERAPHIN

Greetings to you. It is evident that you have a deep concern about karmic issues. Imagine all the different lives you have gone through and all the myriad experiences. These cannot all "fit" into your present brain capacity as a human being in this life, and so indeed you have chosen - from a wealth of possibilities - which experience you wish to improve upon this time around. This means in effect, having a similar experience but DEALING WITH IT BETTER THAN THE LAST TIME. This does not mean DEALING WITH IT PERFECTLY, for the situation is another, and with hindsight there is always a better way to deal with a problem.

THIS IS EXACTLY WHAT YOU ARE DOING HERE, IN FACT; LOOKING AT AN ISSUE WITH HINDSIGHT, and attempting to liberate yourself from that experience so that less "karma" is carried on and over into the next incarnation. This recognition that something may actually REQUIRE a further deeper look into your behaviour might actually not occur during the lifetime itself but IN-BETWEEN. This is where you - with assistance from your guides and other beings - make your decisions of what to experience next. This is not so much of a deleting of negative information forever and ever until the slate is absolutely clean, because in the course of upcoming lives you will - by your own choice - again be challenged by circumstances, and because you have always chosen NEW LEARNING EXPERIENCES you cannot anticipate that your responses will be perfect. The whole essence of this journey IS THAT IT CONTINUES FOREVER: so we are talking about the journey to Paradise AND BEYOND as a continuing and ever improving DEMONSTRATION of optimal behaviour IN THE CIRCUMSTANCES WHICH CAN BE ANTICIPATED BUT NOT METICULOUSLY PLANNED. Especially the reactions of the persons you encounter cannot be meticulously planned. This is more like a steady refining rather than a sense of "OK, now I have dealt with that fully, so I will never have to encounter similar again". This whole path is the journey to Paradise. It is not required to completely resolve everything before starting the journey. If negative behavioural patterns are all eradicated, YOU ARE ALREADY THERE. And as already said, once having achieved Paradise does not mean that you will never be confronted by difficult issues again.

With regard to taking on undesirable karma from others, this can be done, in order to push oneself further up the ladder, so to speak, as in a service rendered. Sometimes this can also be personally damaging, and so this is a question to be considered before the life begins. Regarding planets, Gaia is part of you and you are part of Gaia. Your behaviour affects her whether you are aware of it or not. Any desire you have to help her will surely not go unnoticed.

QUESTION ABOUT TIME

Dear Seraphin. Today many of us feel pressured to accomplish things by a certain time. We also hold ourselves back from doing things because we assume we simply won't have the time to do them. As I understand it, linear time is an illusory concept and that in fact, we are all living in an eternal NOW in which all potentials and possibilities are held. For those of us who find time management challenging, do you have any suggestions so that we can be more effective in accomplishing our action-based goals and find more peace in our lives?

ANSWER FROM SERAPHIN

Greetings. You have identified one of human's main struggles. The concept of time is a HINDERING FACTOR in your view. In general, time is viewed as an ENEMY, preventing you from accomplishing something within a certain framework.

YET WHO HAS PLACE THESE LIMITATIONS? It is you, Beloveds, who have designated that school must finish at 16 or 18, that projects must be completed at a certain date, that there must be an END. But from our perspective, THERE IS NO END, only further development in another sphere or another life.

The seeds sewn at one particular point in time are destined to flourish, if provided with the right conditions. These will appear if they are in alignment with your present learning task, or in alignment with the contribution you are designed to gift your environment and fellow travellers with.

Time is not a preventer but an ENABLER. It is never "too late" to begin on a huge monumental project which will benefit all. In fact, it is always THE RIGHT TIME to do this, even if you are on what you consider to be your "last legs". That seed of greatness with massive potential will sprout later, perhaps with the assistance of a companion or family member, who will NURTURE IT AND BRING IT TO FRUITION.

In this sense, IT IS NEVER TO LATE. I feel I must repeat this, since so many of you on earth have desires and ambitions which are worthy, but are resigned and feel defeated at the great amount of "work" this might entail.

Yet if you are passionate about something, everything will fall into place. This is not a question of having enough time, but of having enough ENTHUSIASM and DEDICATION.

The phrase TIME MANAGEMENT has been invented by humans, not celestials. You feel under pressure to deal with huge amounts of issues and papers in a short period of time, in effect, using time effectively. But you will not be aware of time or its passing or the need to exploit every minute if you are concentrating solely on your passion.

Even if your passion is organisation, sorting through piles of papers or mails WILL BE A JOY rather than something to be dealt with as quickly as possible so that you do not get inundated with more piles of the same.

As you rightly proclaim, the NOW holds great potential and it is for each and every individual to examine if they are living their dream in the NOW or whether they are putting their dream ON HOLD.

<u>**SERAPHIN ANSWERS QUESTIONS ABOUT THE FUTURE**</u>

QUESTION ABOUT FUTURE AGRICULTURE

Dear Seraphin: will we still need food supplements on the new earth? Our soil is depleted of minerals, but are there some simple measures that we could implement even now to heal our soils?

ANSWER FROM SERAPHIN

Greetings to you. Agricultural experts will advise on the replenishing of your soils which are indeed much reduced in their potential to adequately provide. Yet new methods and new strains of food also will enhance this area of development. This, in the end, will provide an abundance of food of such high quality that the word "supplement" will be all but superfluous. In the initial stages, supplements may be necessary as advised by medical staff, yet there will be considerable effort made to make progress towards planting excellent seeds in excellent soil. This is one of the highest priorities.

QUESTION ABOUT STAR SEED CHILDREN

Dear Seraphin: I wonder if all of the young star seeds born onto this earth at the moment will continue here after the great changes, or have some of them only come for a "quick visit"?

ANSWER FROM SERAPHIN

Greetings to you. This is a very complex question as it pertains to a very great number of souls presently arriving for a very diverse number of reasons. The common denominator could be said to be that they all wish to contribute to uplifting consciousness on the planet, but their methods and also their own learning programmes and intentions may DIFFER GREATLY.

Therefore, we must advise you that this is different in each individual case, including the length of their stay here. Indeed, some will have quick visits, and others will have long missions to fulfil.

QUESTION ON HIERARCHIES IN FUTURE SOCIETY

Dear Seraphin: yesterday at work our boss – a "control freak" - was distributing different tasks and responsibilities. How will the hierarchy in future society work? Will it be based on competence? Will all leaders be elected? Will everybody serve? Will organisations be more of an organism?

ANSWER FROM SERAPHIN

Greetings to you. Indeed: there is great wisdom in the statement "LET THE GREATEST AMONG YOU BE YOUR SERVANT". This is what you will gradually be moving towards. Those in leading positions will be there precisely BECAUSE they have an air of calm serenity and BECAUSE their main intent is to serve, NOT BECAUSE THEY WISH TO MAKE MONEY, NOT BECAUSE THEY WISH TO EARN A REPUTATION, NOT BECAUSE THEY WISH TO WIELD POWER AND CONTROL OTHERS.

The seed of destruction in many meetings is that the structures are very strict in the sense that those who are gifted have to "prove themselves" to those higher up in the hierarchy before earning "promotion", elbowing out other people on the way. The whole arena is one of competition and trying to become better than one's colleagues, as opposed trying to co-operate under a single banner of HOW CAN WE OPTIMALLY SERVE.

Those who are "control freaks" are the ones who are worried about delegating responsibility to others for a variety of reasons. Perhaps they have plans which they have personally fashioned and which are their very own "baby". Yet under optimal conditions, the "baby" should be EVERYONE'S CREATION.

Another reason for not wanting to delegate is the fear of losing one's own position or the fear of being shown up and exposed that one is actually not quite as "good" as supposed. In such cases, HONESTY is required, and then there is no need to put on a show or to try and hide what one considers to be "flaws".

The ideal situation is where the "leader" of a group is totally aware of their own strengths and of those of the other people around them. The ideal also is that each person who is entrusted with a task SIGNALS THEIR ABILITY TO DEAL WITH IT, OR ASKS FOR ASSISTANCE IF THEY CANNOT DEAL WITH IT THEMSELVES. This means an ability to admit to what you generally call "weakness", but which may be inexperience or lack of a certain expertise. The "leader" is there to help others grow in their confidence and to assist if necessary.

FLEXIBILITY will be very necessary in your future society. If something is very obviously not working, then the problem must be addressed immediately and changes made. For some of the reasons already mentioned, your organisations tend to slide into chaos or complexities or stressful situations because important issues have not been addressed in time. We look forward to a new and very creative period in the history of your earth, where MONEY or THE NUMBER OF AVAILABLE STAFF will not exert the huge influence which it does today, and where QUALITY will be considered much more important than QUANTITY.

QUESTION ABOUT ROOT CAUSES

Seraphin, you have previously stated that charities and organizations may do some good in alleviating the symptoms, but are ineffective at eradicating root causes. I have a hunch that root causes are not understood and can thus never be tackled, resulting in redundant wheel-spinning and continued ignorance. I estimate that hundreds of thousands of these organizations exist worldwide, many with good intentions, but who are ineffective in executing their stated mission. How might I help these leaders better understand the root causes related to their mission?

ANSWER FROM SERAPHIN

We are delighted at the detailed nature of your question, for indeed it contains much of the answers within it.

Our view of the situation is thus: it may be a very positive factor to train people to use their creative powers, and thus to march with determination yet flexibility towards their chosen goal, yet if this is not accompanied by an alignment with sacred causes, then this energy is sent in a direction which – in the final analysis – does not further the cause of brotherhood of man on this planet. There are many so-called "life coaches" whose intention is to empower individuals and to encourage them into taking matters and in fact their own lives into their own hands, yet the question is: where do they direct this power?

Very often, this is for selfish means in the sense that personal progress and prowess is first and foremost, and one's fellow humans and their plight are secondary.

The "success" of a charity is so often measured by how well known its name may be, how many "resources" it has at its fingertips (or in the bank), or how many employees it has on its registers. Whether the charity itself is really working towards sustainable benefit FOR ALL, or is working in the interests of all (as opposed to working towards the interests of a small group or treating symptoms of a widespread and seemingly incurable phenomenon) is actually what measures its worth.

As you rightly state, there are countless small groups working for change. Very often, their intent is good, but their perspective is limited. There is much to develop on many levels in larger charities. This is perhaps easier to locate, yet here again, the situation is extremely lacking in transparency.

In addition to encouraging creativity, the main thrust must be to intensify investigation into whether their work results in fundamental changes, or if resulting changes are cosmetic or temporary, or just saving someone from the brink for the time being.

The time is arriving when the sugary layer covering the deep holes of dirt will be surgically removed, and those responsible for the topsoil shovelling and beautification of facades will be faced with the full frontage revelation of what they have really done, which is HIDING THE TRUTH. To try and warn such leaders of their actions and such consequences is to show deep compassion, for you will be trying to warn them before the revelations occur, thus preventing the severity of the shock they will receive.

In general, desired perspectives should grow from a local to a national to a cosmic one. Thus will all aspects be included in decisions and thus will they be more effective and grounded in "reality". It will be extremely depressing to discover that the very foundations of one's charitable group are flimsy and in some cases, completely unfounded, or if they are based on lies or false premises.

Critical investigation must be given the highest acclaim. Compassion is already often present in those who commit themselves in this way, so this is not the lacking element. It is the ability to critically assess and to wade through centuries of propaganda which must be part of their efforts.

We know that you have a difficult job ahead and we thank you for the efforts you will be taking to remedy this situation.

QUESTION ON OUR FUTURE CLIMATE

Dear Seraphin: can we expect a more moderate climate on earth, and a lesser tilt, once the big changes are underway?

ANSWER FROM SERAPHIN

Greetings to you. The tilt of your earth is indeed related to the WEIGHT BOURNE BY YOUR MOTHER GAIA, and this is meant in the MENTAL SENSE in that she bears the very great burden of your negative thoughts and actions and abuse over a very long period of time.

YES, ABUSE. You have collectively abused her body and now - during this window of opportunity on many levels - she is choosing to RISE ABOVE THAT NEGATIVITY which has been dragging her down and make her "tilt" (Just as you yourselves might walk slowly, hanging your head in sorrow, if you have been verbally abused, and even more so if you have been physically abused).

The planetary body of Gaia is huge, and while we have experienced teams monitoring her movements, and who will be on call during her rebalancing period, and while they will be able to "tweak" certain situations to aid the process, NOTHING IS SET IN STONE and the progress made will be influenced by many factors.

In addition, THE FASTER YOU LEARN TO CLEAR YOUR NEGATIVITY, THE FASTER YOUR EARTH WILL RECOVER, since you are - as inhabitants - intricately connected. We do anticipate a much-changed landscape and a changed climate for the better, yet the pace of this cannot be determined in advance. The team in charge of this is very experienced and also has considerable technology which can assist.

QUESTION ON HUMAN POTENTIAL

Dear Seraphin: I want to share with you a pertinent thought that came to me recently: WE ARE MORE CAPABLE THAN WE THINK. I have realized that most of us are dormant regarding the capabilities we actually have, which are a gift from God. Could you expand on this?

ANSWER FROM SERAPHIN

Greetings to you and thank you for this extremely important question. I feel that this question needs to be answered right away, although there are others waiting in the "pipeline". I would ask everyone who is reading here to know for a CERTAIN FACT that YOU ARE MUCH MORE CAPABLE THAN YOU THINK. The simple fact that you are reading this, with the intention of acquiring a deeper understanding of your world and its potential and its next step (really we should say "her", as Gaia's body is the earth), is already proof that you are in searching mode and that you have already ACQUIRED a great deal of knowledge, together with the knowledge THAT THERE IS MORE TO LEARN.

If you can convey this to those who suddenly appear in front of you REQUIRING HELP, you can say this with absolute confidence: THAT THERE IS SO MUCH MORE TO LEARN AND SO MANY EXITING NEW PERSPECTIVES TO DISCOVER. This alone will raise their hopes and help them to move forward in a time where they have to LEAVE EVERYTHING BEHIND. I am confident that you will all RISE TO THE OCCASION.

A note here also on the "thought" you suddenly received. It came from A HIGHER PLACE, A PLACE OF HIGHER KNOWLEDGE, A HIGHER SELF which suddenly popped into your mind while actually operating on a "lower" level of consciousness. If such a connection is consciously sought, during quiet moments of the day, it becomes stronger, and thoughts such as this which feel like wise comments which one would not normally say, will become more frequent.

Regarding GIFTS FROM GOD as referenced in your question, we would like to state that these are not "gifts from God" which some people receive and others do not. This would make a division into those who are favoured and those who are victims. The talents and abilities you possess are DEVELOPED BY YOUR-SELVES THROUGH YOUR OWN WORK AND MERIT. In the case of young children who appear to have "special gifts", they bring over special knowledge and capabilities from previous incarnations. While they still have to learn the ropes in this incarnation, it comes to them easily: they have a special affinity with it and can develop rapidly.

QUESTION ABOUT EXCELLENT PREPARATION

Dear Seraphin: I have saved heirloom seeds for over a hundred varieties of vegetable in case they are needed in future. Should they be moved to a safer place? What do I need to undertake to ensure that they are used for the new earth? This matter might seem trivial to the overall picture, but I have been asked to perform certain things and wish to have done so with excellence.

ANSWER FROM SERAPHIN

Greetings to you who are in pursuit of excellence. This is a noble aim. Yet with the limited view you have on the ground, it is difficult to imagine what varieties and perspectives "excellence" in this case might include. There are vast vistas beyond your knowing, and this is necessarily so due to your unique but veiled position on earth in these present circumstances.

To strive and do your best is "excellence" in its earthly form. The provisions which we (the off-planet organisation) have made are indeed all-comprehensive, but this has little to do with the perspective of your personal effort, which is SEEDS SEWN INTO THE MIND OF THE PLANET AND WHICH WILL BENEFIT THE WHOLE PROCESS. Time and care and love and forethought has gone into your preparation of those seeds. This love for the planet demonstrated through such REACHES HER AND HAS A POSITIVE EFFECT. And this is so, even before the seeds are planted.

Imagine that your seeds are left where they are. Perhaps they will float on large waves to another area where the land is very fertile. Thus will they flourish and produce abundant food for others. However, this process involves you LETTING GO of their fate. The seeds, just like yourselves, are guided to THE BEST PLACE TO GROW.

So all we can say in this matter is for you to develop trust in this process - that everything is in the right place at the right time. If you still have questions concerning the seeds, and whether you should personally continue to be their guardian, go within and ask ARE THE SEEDS STILL UNDER MY PROTECTION. Then note what visuals or thoughts arise.

Then ask SHOULD I LEAVE THE SEEDS WHERE THEY ARE? And see what visuals arise. Compare the two and then make your decision accordingly. We will start, as of now, to encourage readers here to move into their own sovereignty in the sense of answering their own questions. We will not simply issue orders of YES, DO THIS or NO, DON'T DO THAT, for this increases reliance on us whereas we are trying to encourage the opposite in a world which has SUFFERED TERRIBLY AS A RESULT OF SUCH DEPENDENCE ON OTHERS.

QUESTION ABOUT AUTHORITY ON THE NEW EARTH

Dear Seraphin: who will hold authority on the new earth?

ANSWER FROM SERAPHIN

Greetings to you. Authority in your world is a very nebulous concept as it mainly rests upon the idea that THOSE WHO HAVE THE POWER HAVE THE AUTHORITY. What we call NATURAL AUTHORITY, which goes hand in hand with a NATURAL AUTHENTICITY, has a very different air and effect. Those with natural authority are not questioned, as they deeply inspire confidence. They immediately cause you to love them. They immediately make you feel appreciated and loved. They do not say many words, but those they utter are like nuggets of gold dropping from their mouths which you will want to run to and pick up. You will hang on their every word, not wanting to miss anything. They will act in alignment with their divinity always, and they will inspire you to do the same. They will encourage you to discover and live your potential in service to others, and in combination with others in a glorious co-creative operation. They will hold back at suitable times and they will speak a firm word when it is necessary. Such will be the "leaders" and authorities in the future on this earth plane. These will be a mixture of members of the celestial hierarchy and their representatives and organisations. It will be very obvious, by their commanding presence, who they are. They will not show signs of "stress" because they will not allow stress to build up. You who read this are asked to improve yourselves and to ever perfect yourselves with each passing day so that you too will emanate this radiance and poise. In this way, YOU WILL CREATE YOUR OWN AUTHORITY.

QUESTION ABOUT EDUCATION AND ART

My question is about new schools on earth.

Is the use of art in the new schools going to be guided by you, Seraphin, and your team? If so, what can we expect in the sense of improved education for children using art as part of the procedure? I am asking this having been born in a part of this world where art is not really important, whereas I would have loved to be in more contact with art.

ANSWER FROM SERAPHIN

Greetings to you. As an inspirational and guiding force, I will stand behind those who wish to implement new creative avenues into the world of learning, yet the specific organisation will be assigned to others. This is a mammoth undertaking - especially as the lack of such teaching is so widespread.

The great delight gained from using one's own creative ideas in all areas will infuse your future days with joy. For inspiration, you can certainly tap into the vast library of possibilities which is available to you through internal connection (you are perhaps familiar with the ROOM OF REQUIREMENT in the Harry Potter films). This means that, if you express your desire and formulate your intentions clearly, in addition to these being intended to help humanity progress during these difficult times ahead, this will be like sending out a signal to your guides and helpers to plant new ideas in your path and to put opportunities in your way.

The speed at which this will occur will take your breath away. Thus will you move forward with exhilaration and enthusiasm, affecting those who walk and work with you, to create wondrous projects together. The word "ART" in its current usage and concept is extremely limited at the present time. It is considered something non-intrinsic to the common mind. Yet - when conceived of as "creativity" - it is intrinsic to the well-being of your world. It is this - FURTHERING THE CREATIVE MIND FRAME WHICH IS EVER EXPANDING AND CHANGING AND FOREVER IN FLOW - which shall be taught on your earth in future. Those deprived areas which have so far not experienced this sort of energy, will burst into bloom.

<u>**SERAPHIN ANSWERS QUESTIONS ON HEALTH**</u>

QUESTION ON THE HUMAN METABOLISM

Seraphin: what should we know about the
nature of the human body?

ANSWER FROM SERAPHIN

We thank you for your question concerning the nature of the human body which is, as always, inextricably related to the nature of the human MIND and its workings. It may be relevant to say that the mind is a very significant DETERMINING FACTOR when considering mechanisms or procedures. Mechanisms do not stand alone, just as atoms and the parts which "compose" the atoms, do not stand alone. They are, as it were, surrounded by what many scientists refer to as "space" but which is actually of substance, and of a substance which vibrates at varying degrees.

If it vibrates quickly, you may regard it as LOVE. If it vibrates slowly, you may regard it as HATE, but whatever the quality, it is the GLUE which holds together. It is not a vacuum, just as your outer space is not a vacuum, but a pressure causing containment. If, for example, an individual is on a spiritual path, continually seeking self-improvement, continually self-reflecting, continually defeating obstacles, meditating and finding answers WITHIN, then the human material WITHIN (including its "needs" and "properties") will change. The quality of the glue inbetween will change - will be more highly charged - and thus will metabolism take an upturn. To vibrate at a very high rate means that you are even invisible to those around you. This may explain to you the presence of - but not the visibility of - angels. There is, affecting your planet at this time, a "quickening factor" which consists of incoming cosmic energies ENCOURAGING UPWARD GROWTH, should an individual be open to this. As a result, the body will change, will be less tolerant of solid food and of animal products. This is a period where you can observe your own bodies and pinpoint or track differences. Here we speak for those with "consciousness" and "awareness". Due to manipulation over centuries, body types also exist which cannot change in this way due to artificial intelligence elements. As you can see, there is so much more to be clarified on your planet.

QUESTION ABOUT RETURNING TO HEALTH

Dear Seraphin: many of us are sick on earth. Often in the west, the best healing systems are well hidden behind a facade of western medical efficiency. I have personally looked at many alternative therapies for my colitis disease, but even the alternatives present a confusing plethora of not so valuable "solutions" to the problem. I have been reduced to trial and error methodology. I have taken interest in Edgar Cayce because he was psychic, and I tend to trust the real psychics. I am sure you will say something wise, so I will just leave the question a little unformed. The real question is how to approach this logically, spiritually and intuitively.

ANSWER FROM SERAPHIN

Greetings to you. You are gradually becoming an expert in sorting through "confusing plethora". The challenges on this planet are extremely grim and do indeed earn the label you have given them. You are to be commended for "entering into the fray", so to speak, and testing every direction TO ITS FULL LIMITS. Only through this sort of process can one really gain the deepest insights which are capable of turning this whole situation around. You are on a learning edge and a steep learning curve of which others can rarely conceive, and while this involves much time and much pain, you shall surely come out of this triumphant and with extremely sharp assessment abilities, in addition to the knowledge that every little detail counts.

You are forced to analyse EVERYTHING which pertains to you and which may or may not have an influence on your health. As such you are a microcosm of that which should be happening on a global scale; as such you are a shining example of how to regain one's footing after being in the depths of despair. You have travelled from death's door back to life, and you can pinpoint exactly what your own contribution has been to that process. This is the IDEAL SCENARIO – where everyone investigates afflictions of all natures in order to understand and turn it around.

The "trial and error" method could be better described as trying to intuitively understand what is happening and why. It is valuable practice in fine-tuning your senses. It is a crash course in self-reliance and it impresses on you the total nature of responsibility. To know all already would be to reduce the learning process to nothing. To discover gradually with many "aha" moments turns the learning process into an adventure which draws ever onwards. Unfortunately, this earth has seen many irresponsible actions performed by its inhabitants, and so you are also influenced by these elements, not entirely of your own making. But here again you are being a role-model for those who may also find themselves in a similar situation. The struggle is long and hard, but every second of contemplation or reassessment is a training of the mind which will serve you extremely well in the future. You have learnt to sort the gold from the dross, so to speak, and so you can make ever more informed choices. Again, we commend you for your journey.

QUESTION ABOUT THE PINEAL GLAND

Seraphin: does the position of the moon affect the activity of the pineal gland?

ANSWER FROM SERAPHIN

Greetings to you, and we see with joy that you are enthusiastic in your search for a higher level of consciousness. It is this – your intention and motivation – which is actually THE MAIN PIVOT and THE MAIN IMPETUS for the awakening process. Yes, there are organs in your body which can reawaken, but this will be less due to the position of the moon (to which far too much power and romantic significance has been ascribed through the ages) and more due to the intensity with which you approach self-improvement, connecting with the divine part within you, and reaching out for new inspiration.

While moving to a new level is aided by incoming cosmic energies, and while cosmic bodies do have a certain influence (just as EVERYTHING exerts a certain influence), you are the main actor in this scenario.

Meditation in the sense of becoming more aware and reflective in places of stillness (and also in places of chaos) as well as a balanced and moderate diet which does not overload the body, are beneficial to the process.

QUESTION ABOUT FOOD QUALITY

Dear Seraphin: could you please tell me whether it is appropriate to continue buying vegetables from a firm which proclaims its love for the earth and for animals, while at the same time using agricultural machines which spray substances made partially of the bones and intestines of dead animals?

ANSWER FROM SERAPHIN

Greetings to you who lives close to the earth and has expressed her deep concern for the processes involved in organic agriculture. This is indeed a deviation from the highly acclaimed achievements of this particular firm. An element of compromise has entered into the scheme of things. This is, in fact, the very great danger which creeps into so many people who have "good intentions", and indeed it is often the case in your corrupted world that QUALITY IS NOT UPHELD.

While this may often be due to money considerations, there are also those who deliberately infiltrate and defile successful enterprises which were originally pure in content. Be aware that you will not – until the changes have occurred – be able to grow or eat a vegetable which is completely untainted. Your soils and air are contaminated and your methods of determining how are also limited. You can attempt to choose to buy less contaminated products, but unless you grow the plants yourselves, you will never actually know what influences they have been subjected to. One of the most powerful element encouraging growth is LOVE. No large firm can claim that.

As regards your choice, this is a case of picking the best, but knowing that none are optimal. We commend you for investigating into these practices. Thus will awareness be raised. There will come a time where ALL ANIMALS WILL BE CONSULTED ABOUT WHETHER THEY CONSENT TO PROVIDING FOOD-STUFFS. Can you conceive of this, children on earth? We leave you with this thought which may propel you to further consider what the optimal solution would be.

QUESTION ABOUT SLEEP

Dear Seraphin: my sleep is restless. Does everybody serve or do some "spiritual work" when the body sleeps, or would some people not experience this at all?

ANSWER FROM SERAPHIN

Greetings to you of the "restless" activity. It is indeed true that you are very much occupied during sleep, as you are during the day. This is, as with all other scenarios, the result of your INTENT TO SERVE. Those who truly express this intent, and seek all possible ways of doing so, will attract such service to them. They will see opportunities everywhere. This is LOVE MANIFEST. However, we consider it just as important to PLAN SPACES TO BREATHE IN. If you do not give yourself breaks during the day, then - as a matter of consequence - you will be forced to take them at night in order to recover. This may make your "night" longer. As always, BALANCE is a keynote here, and you cannot go too far in one direction without having it redressed by the cosmic law of balance. As a result, people who overburden themselves constantly will necessarily develop "burnout syndrome", forcing them to stop.

Your area of activity at night is a continuation of your activity during the day, in a certain sense. Your behaviour, attitudes and intent is not changed simply by crossing the threshold from being awake to being asleep. You carry all this with you. Neither does the barrier from life to "death", as many of you presently prefer to call this transition, mean that you are entering a completely different mind-set. The work on yourselves is done by yourselves, not by a move from A to B.

Those who indulge in low-vibrational activities during the day will continue at this level. You must remember that YOU (and not some outside force or change) are always the protagonists and can decide your future path in whatever realm. Each realm may offer different opportunities, but it is up to you to decide if and how you wish to make use of these opportunities.

Consider your physical life on earth in this physical body: the experience of living in a limited physical vehicle forces the development of the MIND, which can overstep physical limitations. If you can see this, you will perceive that this is a spiritual journey. Thus will you progress throughout the ages and throughout various incarnations, every growing, ever learning, ever putting your acquired knowledge at the service of the DIVINE.

QUESTION ABOUT ORGAN TRANSPLANTS

Seraphin, I wonder what happens to people who get an organ from another person. What happens to the body and the soul of the donor and the receiver of these organs? And what about blood transfusions?

ANSWER FROM SERAPHIN

Greetings to you, and thank you for your question concerning COMPATIBILITY.

You will know, almost instinctively, when you enter a room as a complete stranger, to whom in the group of people at a party you are immediately attracted, in whom you may trust, and who may seem appealing. In the same way, you will immediately sense a feeling of repulsion or disaffection for anyone who seems to be different wavelength. This is not a judgement. It is merely your perception.

Your body is not simply a mechanical machine which is running in a certain way, requiring specific and unchanging physical nourishment. It is influenced, as we just mentioned in the previous answer, by all manner of emotions and experiences undergone by the individual concerned. Thus: imagine that substances or people at a party as mentioned who are seemingly "opposed" to your feeling of well-being, ACTUALLY ENTER YOUR BODY. In actual fact, their vibration already does, even if you are physically separate.

So, if the blood or organ of another person ACTUALLY ENTERS YOUR BODY ON A PHYSICAL LEVEL you can imagine that there may be a grave reaction of shock. This cannot be compared to an hour or so spent in the company of those you do not agree with. This means a LIFETIME OF CONTINUOUS ADJUSTMENT TO SOMETHING NECESSARILY FOREIGN TO YOURSELF. Do not underestimate the traumatic and permanent effects this can have on your psyche, and thus on your body. To assimilate something completely foreign into your own body is be in a continual state of confrontation, and thus of weakness. It equates to massive and continuous irritation – quite the opposite of the "live-saving" aspect which is so frequently presented to you in order to support organ donating and also – unfortunately - the illegal organ trade.

In view of new possibilities of growing organs from stem cells and other technologies not yet fully disclosed in your present physical realm, your present methods – combined with the inhumanity which these processes involve – is something we view from afar with such deep pain, and many such operated persons feel that pain too, to say nothing of the pain of the donors if not yet fully "dead" (though once the "soul", the eternal part of oneself, has left the physical body, the physical pain is over). Yet it is pain which will open your eyes, little ones on earth, as in so many areas which involve violence, exploitation and corruption.

Ingesting flesh is another part of this problem. You actually ingest matter very similar to your own. It involves killing the owner/inhabitant of the flesh, it includes the violence, it involves the taking away of the life flow. All this information is fed into you. For living cells with a conscience (of which your body is formed) this is indeed a traumatic event – to deal with their own kind. We leave it to you to decide whether you want to continue this behaviour and whether it benefits you, humanity or the environment in any way.

QUESTION ABOUT EAR TONES

Seraphin, I have a question about ear tones. I have often heard ear tones that last for about 10 seconds. Sometimes the everyday noise will go quiet, for few seconds, and then the ear tone will appear and then fade away, with the background noise going back to normal. The most frequent time that I heard ear tones was the week of the big New Zealand earthquake a few years ago. Can you please give me some information as to what is the true cause of ear tones, and about the pitch of the frequency of the tone I am hearing.

ANSWER FROM SERAPHIN

Greetings to you of the GREAT AURAL SENSITIVITY. Your increased sensitivity is the reason for your increased hearing. The vibrations which run around the earth and indeed form part of her various mental and emotional bodies are extremely complex and in fact pick up and absorb any abnormalities – including earth movements, explosions or other tumultuous events – which enter her "subconscious", as it were.

The more you align yourself with earth and her feelings, including her sufferings, the more clearly this sound will RISE ABOVE those which are within your range of normality, even cutting them out for a period.

The sounds you are hearing may be related to quakes or any other large event, since there is also a process of cumulation, and each event affects the next, resulting in a very heavy burden which your planet presently carries, causing her to tilt. We could say that you are perceiving the cumulative effect of her pain when it gets too much for her.

As such, you are what is called an "empath", and each empath will notice and feel the signs in different ways. The precise pitch is not an issue here, rather the frequency with which you hear indicates the seriousness of the situation.

To go into sympathy with the earth is a sign of great compassion and understanding, yet to take on the suffering may also mean an overload of your own circuits resulting in physical damage. We ask you to keep this in mind and to survey your own condition of health.

QUESTION ABOUT VEGETARIANISM

On the new earth, Seraphin, will there be a need to be vegetarian or will there still be slaughter houses working to kill animals for food? If so, who will want to slaughter animals on the new world? Will this be a very slow change? Or will there be surrogate meat?

ANSWER FROM SERAPHIN

Greetings to you. We are delighted with your question WHO WILL WANT SLAUGHTER ANIMALS ON THE NEW WORLD? Who indeed. There are presently many earth inhabitants who slaughter animals on a daily basis and who eat animals on a daily basis. The best cases of improvement in any society have never been the result of saying THIS IS NOT ALLOWED, but the result of turning the focus away in another more humane direction. In this case, this will mean PROVIDING ALTERNATIVES wherever possible. You will be surprised at the variety of alternatives. You will be surprised at the quality and high vibration of the food you will be allowed to choose from, since all this food will be grown UNDER OPTIMAL CONDITIONS and WITH LOVE.

Following a teaching period, I suspect there will be very few who will not be able to recognise the abhorrent acts they have committed, and there will be very few who wish to perpetrate this. However, the whole situation is in the hands of the celestial organisers, but you can rest assured that very strong steps will be taken to deter same, and that they will do everything in their power to increase enthusiasm for vegetarian food.

Those who live on the planet must reach a certain level of "love" vibration, and this generally means NOT DESIRING TO KILL.

QUESTION ABOUT HEALTH

Dear Seraphin: can you please give me some information about what blood pressure is ideal? It has changed over the years, and now pills are being given to redress imbalances.

ANSWER FROM SERAPHIN

Greetings to you. You are rightly very concerned about "health". It must always be remembered that physical health is extremely closely connected with mental and emotional health. To oversee this forms grounds for erroneous decisions. To ignore this is to fall into the position of NO PERSONAL RESPONSIBILITY and to do this is to become victim to those who are only too ready to exploit you in all ways for their own personal benefit. This makes you (or anyone who refuses to take on responsibility for self) susceptible to the LAW OF THE JUNGLE. Instead, you should see YOURSELVES as the REGULATING POWER. Those who give their regulating powers over to pills are, in a way, giving themselves up. It is this regained strength and confidence in yourselves and your own abilities to ASSESS, CHANGE, ADAPT and SELF REVIEW which our messages have concentrated on over time. Our way is the difficult, less trodden path. Generally, accepting a doctor's prescription after a 5-minute consultation is the easy way out.

While I personally have no expertise in the medical field, I can say that ALL IS CONNECTED. To see the heart and its functioning as isolated from the whole (and to see the results of your actions as isolated from the actual behaviour which caused it) is to have only a partial view of what is really going on.

To be connected to all means having a relationship with all and having an overview of all, and in the medical sphere this means a HOLISTIC APPROACH. It is entirely possible to ask yourselves WHAT IS MY HEART TRYING TO TELL ME or WHAT ARE MY LEGS TRYING TO TELL ME and to have a conversation with this part of yourself during meditation. It is up to yourselves to seek the answers, to discover WHY your bodies are not in balance, to seek out the grey areas in your integrity, to search for that which clouds your perceptions, to discover areas which you usually regard as unpleasant, to air those issues which you dread or of which you are secretly ashamed. ALL YOUR THOUGHTS AND ACTIONS ARE REFLECTED IN YOUR BODIES: all cells have memories which they store. Just as you are living, YOUR CELLS ARE LIVING. They experience ALL YOUR EMOTIONS, INCLUDING THOSE YOU COVER UP OR SUPPRESS (in fact, ESPECIALLY THOSE) and as such they will REACT either favourably or unfavourably.

In your fast track lives, your bodies are often overlooked, yet they are a reflection of the inner workings of your minds and they are attempting to reach your conscious mind. If all else fails to get your attention, they will STOP WORKING and some sort of blockage or extreme condition will actually force you to stop. This has been christened BURN OUT syndrome, whereas it could actually be called THE SYNDROME OF NOT LISTENING TO YOUR BODY AND REFUSING TO ACCEPT THAT IT IS A REFLECTION OF YOUR MIND, OR LACK OF MIND GROWTH.

So, whereas emergency measures sometimes have to be taken to deal with critical conditions, these will only keep symptoms at bay and will do nothing to counteract the cause, which is yourselves. Those who have high "pressure" can ask themselves whether they, like the supposed actions of the blood, are forcing or pressurising themselves in any direction, irrespective of collateral damage. This, like so many other things, is a question of BALANCE and of how you run your lives on a daily basis.

The most poignant things missing in your lives are the CONNECTION TO THE DIVINE and the MEDITATIVE PAUSES which can offer information to keep you on track, which can regulate your pace (AND THUS YOUR HEART) and which can provide you with the wisdom to change direction if necessary, so that your work (and here we mean your service to humanity) can continue at a steady rate which is suitable to you and your needs, so that optimal benefit can be drawn from your present incarnation on your upward spiritual journey.

QUESTION ABOUT CAUSES OF WEAK IMMUNE SYSTEMS

My question is a 'medical' one, as my job at the local hospital has brought a lot of contemplation forth during my daily work. I see an increasing number of cases of so called autoimmune 'diseases' and I wonder if these attacks by patients' own immune systems on their bodies are in fact caused by lack of self-love or self-forgiveness?

ANSWER FROM SERAPHIN

Greetings to you, and thank you for dedicating much of your time to others. This we appreciate. The helping professions are generally not appreciated as much as they could be. However, the optimal situation would be that EVERYONE helps themselves rather than becoming weak and requiring outside help.

Those who find themselves in a state of weakness, or even in the position where their own body seems to be attacking itself, should know that this is the fruit of a seed sewn in the past. Often this is the result of repetitive abusive behaviour to self. This can take many forms. It can mean biting your lip every time someone says something abusive to you. It can be the alcohol you pour into your body on a regular basis. It may be a daily decision not to go outside for a walk or partake in some sort of movement / sport. These small daily decisions turn into habits which are sometimes very difficult to drop.

Love of self is not really encouraged in this sense. You are encouraged to look good, present yourself as being confident, well-heeled and solvent, and this may involve many sacrifices which are not beneficial to your mind or your body. Often the needs of the body and self are ignored by yourselves, and thus your mind runs ROGUE and overrides other considerations. And if your mind runs ROGUE it is only question of time before the cells in your body run ROGUE too, ignoring the needs of the other cells. To look at those who are weak and who require support, this will not be the first thought in your mind. Your first thought may be that they are deserving of your compassion and help. This may be a chance for you to exercise compassion, yes, but those who are in a weak state of health are nevertheless demonstrating in some way the CUMULATIVE EFFECT OF THOUSANDS OF DECISIONS made during every day of their lives.

"Forgiveness" can only be truly felt if one truly understands WHAT ONE HAS ACTUALLY DONE. If it is accepted that you have been the cause of your physical state, then you can truly forgive yourself and send "love" to your body. This will have an effect. However, if you continue to blame outward sources, this process cannot take place.

QUESTION ABOUT HEALING

Dear Seraphin: as energetic beings experiencing a great deal of stress and suppressed emotion which manifests in disease, chronic negative emotional states, and a vast amount of other issues, we humans all require some degree of balancing, healing, and integration in order to more fully align with our eternal selves. Some people approach healing by bringing awareness to the "root" of the initial trauma and processing it through hypnosis, meditation or similar modalities. Others choose to not put their attention on the negative by practicing positive thinking, "breathing through it", "living in the now" and "letting go," for instance. I believe that all such techniques for healing are valid and one's soul will ultimately guide them to the best combination of therapeutic practices, but I would like to know if you could generally address the effectiveness and usefulness of healing with these more "profound" and more "topical" techniques, and if bringing awareness or acceptance to the root of something is the only way to truly heal an unhealthy core program/belief/pattern. And because what happens internally is reflected in the external world, could you expand on the ideal methods of bringing awareness of global atrocities, so that they too may be processed and purged at the level of the collective consciousness?

ANSWER FROM SERAPHIN

Greetings to you. In this we can only repeat that this is a personal journey of choice, and as such, inner intuition will guide to suitable methods of therapy. However, it may well transpire that after repeated efforts, an individual will realise that the chosen method, considered after much deliberation, and perhaps involving the spending of much money, was not the "right" one after all.

However, it is the "right" one for the learning process involved. This is why we emphasise the personal aspect of this.

The other point we wish to make is that attempting to treat the symptoms of a problem (and this may well be achieved through relaxation, "breathing through it" or whatever method) will not eradicate the problem/illness itself. It is indeed necessary to go to the root of a problem in order to erase it completely. And it is not possible to erase something completely without a very long and hard look at your behaviour.

The root of a physical problem is always a psychological one. It is this thought / concept which is so often rejected in a world based very much on materialist principles. There are methods of reaching that root. It requires effort and a very searching look at events in one's life and HOW you reacted to those, and HOW YOU CONTRIBUTED TO THOSE, for everything you experience IS YOUR OWN CREATION.

All those suffering intensely will have an intense reaction to this statement, rejecting it outright. If this is the case, they do not wish to leave the position in which they receive sympathy. They think they are entitled to sympathy in a never-ending stream. Yet their role is another: to come to terms with their role as a CREATOR. The transition from victim to creator is massive. Yet if one can easily identify all events in life in which one was angry, sad, and supposedly caught in the trap of another, we say THINK AGAIN and approach every situation as the CO-CREATOR OF THAT SITUATION. Realise also that your personal unseen guides are sometimes forced to help you in very "unorthodox" ways, in order to prevent total self-destruction, which may result in a minor injury or disappointment of some sort. Realise that there are all sorts of forces at play here, but their INTENTIONS ARE GOOD. To understand this is to set yourselves free.

On the global level, this applies also. While charities and other organisations may succeed to a degree in reducing unpleasant situations around the world, THEY DO LITTLE TO ERADICATE THE CAUSES OF THE PROBLEMS. This is why all work which digs very deeply into the multiple layers and complexities of violent and abusive scenarios is SO IMPORTANT. Much is still undercover. And when the truth is finally revealed it will be this which results in the greatest changes.

QUESTION ABOUT ALLERGIES

Dear Seraphin: over this last decade I have developed an allergy to perfume, which is not surprising because many contain chemicals. I have three cousins who are allergic to certain food substances and animals. Are allergies the result of our highly polluted world, or is there a different reason on an emotional or mental level?

ANSWER FROM SERAPHIN

Greetings to you. First, it must be said that I am not on the medical team involved with earth's inhabitants at this time, yet it is surely clear that the rise in irritants in your food systems and atmosphere will be increasingly more destructive to those of sensitive constitution, and this can be transferred from mother to child. Thus there are outer conditions which endanger health.

There are also inner conditions which "allow" intruders in the sense of unwanted bacteria or viruses to enter and ride the body freely. The parallel here would be, on a psychological level: why would you let someone or something enter your sphere, although you know that they will have an adverse influence? Or: why do you succumb to other's wishes, when they do not correspond with your own. Or: why are you easily exploited by others? Or - and this is the real crux of the matter - why have you abandoned the idea of your own worth and your own divinity?

Perhaps that sense of self has never been developed, or has never been entertained. Now is the time to counteract this feeling of unworthiness and to discover that there is another path and that it is also time to stop the path of destruction which affects your lives, your surroundings and also YOUR BODIES.

The skin, where many allergies show a strong reaction, is actually a barrier between outside and inside the body. This barrier is necessary for protection, and it has been blighted by all sorts of physical elements as well as - on another level - propaganda and distortion of truth. If the barrier is intact, you cannot be exploited or hurt. If the barrier is intact you can see everything clearly, not as a victim, but objectively. It is towards this stance that you should try to progress. Then will the allergies recede.

SERAPHIN ANSWERS QUESTIONS ABOUT THE EARTH

QUESTION ABOUT NATURE AS A SYSTEM

Seraphin: would you say that nature is over-romanticised?

ANSWER FROM SERAPHIN

We thank you for your questions which are the product of a lively and inquisitive mind in search of the truth. The "truth" has many layers and many perspectives.

Nature, as you have well noted, is not to be "romanticized". It is a system which is – like your human society – either in balance or not. And, in fact, all systems correlate with each other and influence each other, because every word and action of all living beings is fed into the earth's genetic mind and has been stored there for thousands and thousands of years. This "pool" of information" is how animals retrieve their instructions, how frogs know what to do and how to develop, and indeed how bees know how to communicate and how to organise themselves.

The human system – which has been devised to take on the more developed souls as a way of education - has the worthy aim of PERFECTING THE HUMAN SOUL. Yet during the past thousands of years, this progress has not moved forward but has moved backward many times, resulting in the complete decimation of civilisations which considered themselves "developed", but which actually caused their own downfall.

You have seen how bees also, in some cases, cause their own downfall, or at least cause the downfall of some of their comrades. This cannot be attributed to the bees themselves but to the IMMORAL ATTITUDES OF THE HUMAN RACE whose members (many of whom have been through the whole evolutionary process, including incarnation as animals) should actually have left the "killing each other" stage behind.

But this is not the case. You only have to see the number of wars presently occurring on your planet to realise this.

This information is ALSO IN EARTH'S GENETIC MIND, which is akin to a huge computer to which all living beings have access. YOUR COLLECTIVE VIOLENCE THUS AFFECTS THE ANIMAL WORLD.

Once connections have been re-established to other spiritually more advanced worlds, you will see that their animals no longer fear for their life or have the desire to kill others. Nor do they develop stings or poison.

Unfortunately, you cannot yet observe such wonderful scenes.

You are presently restricted to observing the nature which exists on your planet, with all its "imperfections". But even this is capable of ELEVATING YOU TO ANOTHER SPHERE, where you can wonder at the perfection of a rose, or wonder at the way the bees collectively care for their young and produce honey (and if the honey was not taken away from them at regular intervals, then perhaps they would change rapidly too…).

We thank you for your interest, Seraphin

QUESTION ON PESTS

Dear Seraphin: when Earth is renewed, what is going to happen to roaches, ants, rats or other "pests" that we consider to be a nuisance? When they infect our house, we sometimes kill them to get rid of them, but I tend to feel sorry for them because they are living creatures as well, and sometimes I feel that I am not doing the right thing. Can you comment on that, please.

ANSWER FROM SERAPHIN

Greetings to you, and thank you for this important question. You (and all others - we speak generally here) are ONE with the animals you perceive of as "pests" in the sense that the aggression demonstrated by them is a reflection of the global mind to which all have contributed. Think how many inhabitants of earth have simply taken away the habitat of animals - for example through logging - for their own use. Thus seeds of violence and selfishness are sewn into the "morphogenetic" field.

If forced into a small area - together with less protection and food - animals will go into increased self-defence mode. This is a very general description, but do not underestimate how humans have contributed to the huge imbalance in nature on many levels, and this will not simply continue without suffering the consequences.

The memory of all actions are HELD ON THE ONE EARTH and are part of the SAME ONE SYSTEM. All this is low-level spiritual activity, if I may be allowed to call it thus. What is approaching is an INCREASE from this low-level vibration to a higher one. Whether human or animal, ADAPTATION WILL HAVE TO BE MADE. Otherwise it is not possible to continue here. Note also that there are experts in charge of decisions in this area which includes the restoring of BALANCE in nature.

Concerning the killing of pests; your compassion is commendable but it is also necessary to deal with encroaching behaviour if this causes largescale damage or threatens hygiene. On a mental level, this is also recommendable. Examine carefully which behaviours are threatening your mental hygiene and seek to root them out. Here again, we are attempting to demonstrate that everything is connected. It is also possible to go into meditation and ask what mental trait the "pests" correspond to within yourself. Consideration of this will also have an effect on outer circumstances, as is always the case. AS WITHIN, SO WITHOUT.

QUESTION ABOUT LEY LINES AND SACRED BUILDINGS

Dear Seraphin: many sacred buildings have been erected over ley lines. But with future earth changes, I imagine that ley lines will also change. I wonder if we will then erect more buildings that will enhance Gaia's wellbeing, providing more balance and healing. I am also wondering if it might be possible to make underwater gardens in the oceans, since half of the planet is under water.

ANSWER FROM SERAPHIN

My greetings to you of the active imagination. Your very questions indicate through their ingenuity and perspective that you have inside you the seeds for new developments and places, whether on land or underwater. The eventual aim of all such activities is to enhance your world so that it qualifies for the attribute SACRED. The quality of your creations will make it so.

Much will be changed on the surface of the earth, meaning a general reshuffle of avenues of energy, points of axis and the position of the equator etc., and this is in effect up to Gaia to decide how the cards fall, to use one of your earthly expressions.

Yet this is not simply a haphazard and perchance falling of cards in a non-predetermined manner, since all developments will be closely monitored and tweaked if necessary by fleet staff in order to make things run more smoothly. This may involve "detonating" or setting off certain movements in order to stall bigger ones.

It will take some time before such activities have ceased to the point where it will be possible to build absolutely "safe" sacred places. As has been mentioned before, what is known as a "morontial temple" will be established. This will be the main "sacred place" for the time being. Other sacred places from long ago may also re-emerge from the sea. An increase in underwater gardening will be possible when agitated oceans become calm.

QUESTION ABOUT COMMUNICATION WITH NATURE

Seraphin: will it be common to communicate with nature in future - with plants and animals - to see how we can better help them? We could ask plants where they would like to be planted, or what nourishment they require, or what music or colours they might like. Some of the forest trees at the back of my house must have some interesting stories to tell. The deer too. Could Gaia let us know what would be pleasing to her?

ANSWER FROM SERAPHIN

Greetings to you. Like all increases in abilities, the realisation of one's own potential, together with the purposeful application of energy into learning and practicing, will enable you to move into new and exciting directions. There are no sudden waving of wands in this regard. However, present energies affecting the planet will assist this upward movement of intending to develop, just as they will bring the very opposite to a screeching halt. The path you choose to follow will be supported if it is to bring more understanding between different portions of the One, and to bring more communication and understanding between humans and animals - all living creatures on the same plane. This is indeed a worthy commitment.

Those who are already sensitive to this in the sense of telepathic ability, will see their sensitivity increase. The intent of the person concerned is of primary importance. I would remind you that there are those who have demonstrated such abilities in the past, but who have specifically asked them to be removed, as they could not cope with the results such abilities bring. This is a question of responsibility. Some have not been ready to accept the responsibility which goes with this. On planets of a higher spiritual level there are indeed channels of telepathic communication between all species, but this state will not suddenly appear on earth. It is something to be moved towards gradually. Your increase in love and respect for nature, and the intrinsic knowledge worldwide that all living beings FEEL, HAVE EMOTIONS and are LIVING CREATURES, is the first step on this journey. Without this prerequisite realisation, communication cannot proceed.

QUESTION ABOUT CREATING GARDENS

My question is about creating gardens.

In the higher worlds, how alike and how different are gardens from what we create here? I know that much of what we consider to be beautiful gardens here is about controlling nature as opposed to working with it. Will the removal of "dark energies" from the planet free up our thinking so that we create gardens in ways we cannot at present imagine?

ANSWER FROM SERAPHIN

Greetings to you. You have GREAT DORMANT POTENTIAL. The very nature of your question demonstrates the knowledge - perhaps not entirely out in the open, but dormant and waiting - which will transform your earth into a GLOBAL GARDEN.

Controlling nature is indeed a practice which has taken over in all areas of agriculture and other areas also. Much of this is done to increase produce, and is done under the auspices of PROFIT. This major aspect will cease as the focus turns away from profit-making and accumulating large amounts of money towards co-operative living IN A WAY IN WHICH THE EARTH IS LOVED AND PROTECTED.

If you investigate the ways that nature has been "controlled" over the centuries, such as the building of enormous dams on large rivers, you will observe how - ultimately - these measures may have served short term objectives but leave long-term issues in their wake, which in turn need more "correcting".

This is the great CORRECTING TIME, and to reinforce harmonious living WITH nature as opposed to AGAINST NATURE is a very important part of the process. It will no longer be permitted nor possible to build islands in the sea for luxury homes. The seas will be agitated, and Gaia will have her period of adjustment which involves rebalancing.

In the same sense, you as a global population must rebalance, reducing excesses and respecting natural resources. When this concern for the preservation of the beauties of nature is truly part of the desires of all inhabitants, then can you start to jointly create gardens which flourish both for the delight of the eye, and for the delight of the palate.

Permaculture will be observed rather than the monoculture developed presently. Those with expertise in this will come to the fore and present their guidelines in this area. Thus, it is not only the removal of dark energies but the rise in consciousness of those remaining which will bring about change.

QUESTION ABOUT MEDICAL HELP
Will we receive medical help in the new world, Seraphin?
Will missing limbs be able to grow back? There are a lot of sick people who will be needing medical attention.

ANSWER FROM SERAPHIN

Greetings to you, and thank you for your concern for those who presently suffer affliction in the form of disease. We can reassure you that medical surveillance is one of the very first things which you will experience, and we can also reassure you that everything in our power will be applied – including much more developed medical technology than that with which you are presently familiar.

As always, the attitude of the patient is an essential component in the healing process. If a patient is asked if he or she wishes to heal, and if they cooperate, the process will begin. If the patient is not willing to change or to work on certain aspects of their behaviour or emotional state, affecting their emotional bodies, then the physical body cannot move forward into healing.

This is also the case on your world at the moment. They are doctors who heal cancer who first ask the patient "DO YOU WISH TO HEAL?" They do not proceed unless the patient answers in the affirmative. This is an essential part of the process. As in every area, the intent of the person involved is essential, and their willingness to change is required. Failing this, any treatment which is completed is merely an eradication of symptoms. The "disease" remains and will raise its head again.

Concerning medical procedures regarding new limbs, I am not on the medical staff, so not qualified to make pronouncements here, especially as every case is different, but you will be very surprised at the new possibilities.

GRATITUDE

Profound gratitude to Seraphin for answering these questions. Names, other personal identification tags and references to complex material have been removed for the sake of clarity and understanding.

Rosie Jackson.

ABOUT THE AUTHOR

ART - MUSIC - SERAPHIN MESSAGES - SEMINARS

Rosie Jackson is an author, artist, composer and the founder of *The Spiritual Revolution Project*. This encompasses paintings, music, videos, books and seminars to develop self-awareness. Teaching spiritual principles to promote consciousness, her music and art are powerful catalysts of spiritual uplift. Her *Unity Tarot* illustrates the transformation of 100 global villagers in 2 large paintings and 100 written biographies.

Since 2010, Rosie Jackson has been receiving telepathic messages and visions from the angel, Seraphin. These communications urge us to protect our earth and show us how paradise on earth can be achieved. The messages are presently available in English, German, Italian, Spanish, Dutch and Korean.

Born in England, Rosie Jackson studied German and French and qualified as a teacher. She has worked as an instructor in China, and as a translator, designer and editor for publishing houses and companies in Europe. She now works freelance as an artist, author and spiritual teacher in Germany and Italy.

rosie@rosiejackson.de.

OTHER PUBLICATIONS BY ROSIE JACKSON

The Complete Seraphin Messages: Volume 1
ISBN 978-3-751976-72-5 (Seraphin Series: Book 4)

The Complete Seraphin Messages: Volume 2
ISBN 978-3-75198150-7 (Seraphin Series: Book 5)

The Complete Seraphin Messages: Volume 3
ISBN 978-3-75190001-0 (Seraphin Series: Book 6)

The Complete Seraphin Messages: Volume 4
ISBN 978-3-752 643275 (Seraphin Series: Book 7)

Seraphin's Spirituality School
ISBN 978-3-749485-84-0 (Seraphin Series: Book 1)

The World will become Peaceful, Beautiful and Abundant
ISBN 978-3-751920-66-7 (Seraphin Series: Book 2)

The Peace Parables
ISBN 978-3-750441-51-4 (Seraphin Series: Book 3)

The Absolutely Amazing Activity Book
ISBN 978-3-8370-0238-6

***Wie das Schweinchen Prinzessin Prunella
das Lachen lernte***
ISBN 978-3-749428-85-4

***Ich bin Lebendigkeit:
Eine Reise zu mehr Authentizität, Kraft und Freude***
ISBN 978-3937883-32-8

WEBSITES

BUY ART PRINTS:
https://www.artflakes.com/en/s?search=Rosie+Jackson

MAIN WEBSITE:
www.rosiejackson.de

MUSIC ALBUM:
https://rjspirit100.bandcamp.com/album/songs-for-the-era-of-light-and-life

SEMINARS:
http://www.rosie-jackson.de/revolution/Seminar_Termine.html

INSTAGRAM:

https://www.instagram.com/rjspirit100/

THE SPIRITUAL REVOLUTION PROJECT:
http://www.rosie-jackson.de/revolution/Projekt_und_Vision.html

MUSIC/ART VIDEOS:
https://www.youtube.com/cha-nel/UCMCeJnqJ9Y7hqAExYmm9iKA

Rosie Jackson

AN ANGEL SPEAKS
SERAPHIN'S SPIRITUALITY SCHOOL
YOUR DIVINE ROLE:
CREATING AN ERA OF PEACE

ISBN 978-3-749485-84-0. 2019. 292 pages

Seraphin is an angel who send us messages of hope and inspiration, as well as practical advice. Our world requires a drastic makeover, and this will be fueled by a universal change of heart, by widening our perspectives, and by reconnecting to the divine core within us, which impels us to develop our skills in service to humanity.

Seraphin's statements provide remarkable insights, provoke intense reflection, and challenge our limited viewpoint. With great clarity, he points out the necessity for radical change, while knowing that we have the power to implement it. The messages in this book were received telepathically by Rosie Jackson.

This collection of 111 Seraphin Messages has 5 purposes. The first chapter, "Messages from the other side" encouraging readers to start a writing journey, contacting their unseen guides and "downloading" information relevant to their particular task on earth. As your spiritual abilities progress, you will increase in confidence, and you will become a source of inspiration for others.

Secondly, the chapters entitled "Your divine purpose", "Transcending your past", "Creating your future", and "Your relationships", intend to help readers along the spiritual path, assisting them to develop potential, achieve excellency, and use these skills and knowledge for the benefit of all.

Chapter 3, "Preparing for transition", provides advice on how to deal with the intense times ahead. Due to our present position in the photon belt, our planet is showered with highly powered cosmic energies.

These create enormous change, supporting everything of divine nature, and exposing that which is not.

Fourthly, the chapters on rebuilding our world offer instructions on how to address practical problems. They also highlight which qualities we should manifest in order to maintain peace, beauty and abundance on our world.

Fifthly, the goal of the very last chapter, "Reconnecting to the universe", aims to increase our awareness of our galactic neighbours who lovingly observe us. After millennia of "disconnection", we will finally resume our membership of the cosmic family.

Rosie Jackson

**THE ABSOLUTELY AMAZING ACTIVITY BOOK OF
SNAKES, STARS AND SNOWBALLS**
FURTHERING CREATIVE EXPRESSION
IN CHILDREN FROM THE AGE OF 7 UP

ISBN: 978-3-8370-0238-6

Each of these 80 pages presents a story, idea, or situation which stimulates children's imagination through questions, suggestions or invitations to wonder what happens next. The pictures they then draw are subconscious images of their inner world, feelings and desires, thus providing their carers with a valuable window to their soul.

Once children are accustomed to expressing their own emotions and needs, they are better able to assess themselves and others on the path towards mutual understanding and peace. Like SNAKES they can shed their old skins, like SNOWBALLS they can move on and grow, reaching more and more towards the stars.

Rosie Jackson

THE WORLD WILL BECOME
PEACEFUL, BEAUTIFUL AND ABUNDANT
A compact instruction manual:
150 ways to improve our world

ISBN 9783751920667.196 pages

Our desecrated, ravaged earth requires massive overhaul. WHAT CAN WE DO? This instruction book for individuals and groups presents 150 methods of making the world peaceful, beautiful and abundant. They focus on personal, social, cultural, environmental and global RESPONSIBILITIES. Most important, however, is the recognition of our divine responsibilities:

"We are the drop of water in a polluted ocean. We are a genetically manipulated seed planted in a field which has been doused with artificial fertiliser. We are a small tender plant strangled by rampant weeds. We are a million stars in a far-flung galaxy.

If we can take on these roles, we will ask WHY and search for solutions. If we are in polluted water, we will seek METHODS OF PURIFICATION. If we are a genetically manipulated seed, we will seek METHODS TO REVERSE ADVERSE PROGRAMING. If we are planted in contaminated soil, we will seek METHODS TO REGENERATE NATURALLY. If we are strangled by weeds, we will seek METHODS OF CLEARING THE MENTAL JUNGLE. And if we are a million stars, we will be encouraged to LIVE OUR INFINITE POTENTIAL AND SPREAD LIGHT ETERNALLY".

These poetic as well as practical pearls of wisdom have been provided by the angel Seraphin, and have been received telepathically between 2009 and 2020 by the author and artist, Rosie Jackson.

Rosie Jackson

THE PEACE PARABLES:
HOW THE FOOL BECAME GOD,
AND OTHER STORIES

ISBN 9783750441514, 140 pages

What do the stories with the titles INSIDE THE MARBLE and THE ROOF and THE EMERGENCY BRAKE have in common? Like the other 53 stories in this volume, they are "peace parables" because they urge us to improve our behaviour, not only for our own benefit, but for the common good, enabling us to co-create a peaceful world. Most of these parables are descriptions of visions received during meditation by the author and artist, Rosie Jackson. Some are adaptations of messages received telepathically from the angel, Seraphin.

One of the most famous storytellers is the soul we call Jesus. Parables are an excellent way of teaching, as they entertain and educate people of various paths simultaneously, without raising an accusing finger. No one is addressed personally. It is up to readers to draw their own conclusions. All these parables are designed to assist readers on their spiritual journey, opening up new vistas, opportunities and directions. The stories provide insights, shake up superstitions, encourage heroic acts, expose corruption, pinpoint our enslaved mentalities, reveal our debilitating dependence, revive our dormant creative powers, invite reassessment of the "status quo", reveal downward spirals, discourage materialism, inspire love of nature and foster true values.

The stories entertain and educate, urging us to search for better solutions, to increase compassion and recognise our interconnection. They illuminate dangerous domino effects, and expose our narrow-mindedness and blind allegiance. These stories prepare us to be flexible in the face of great change, and force us to reflect upon our LIFE'S PURPOSE.

THE SPIRITUAL REVOLUTION PROJECT

In 2005, the artist Rosie Jackson made a mental note of the fact that different people were always sending her the same text which began "If the world was a village of 100 people", and she decided that this was not coincidence, but divine synchronicity. Using the global statistics in this text (concerning nationality, religion, living conditions etc.) she invented 100 "global villagers" – each of whom represented 1% of the global population - and wrote their biographies. Then she depicted these "global villagers" in a 5-metre-long painting entitled THE WORLD-REALITY, illustrating the whole range of human problems on earth.

But having done this, she felt she could not just leave it at that, so she spent another 2 years considering how each of the 100 global villagers could turn their lives around if they pursued a certain "positive" quality (such as respect, gratitude or compassion). Then she painted the 100 figures anew, depicting their transformation, in another large painting entitled THE WORLD-VISION. The 100 positive qualities act as the catalyst for the SPIRITUAL REVOLUTION which can transform our world into paradise. The 100 biographies all have a "happy end" and include 10 pertinent questions, and this now forms the UNITY TAROT which is used as the basis for Rosie's seminars.

100 TRANSFORMATIVE QUALITIES IN THE UNITY TAROT

What qualities must we develop to ensure peace and become "one"? The UNITY TAROT offers 100 "positive" qualities which can serve as a point of orientation. The more we voluntarily and conscientiously adhere to them out of love for ourselves and our fellow humans, the faster we will move towards harmonious living. The transformation of the 100 global villagers does not lie in increased material wealth but in increased demonstration of these positive qualities.

SPIRITUAL REVOLUTION SEMINARS

In the course of these seminars, participants encounter everything which separates them from others (culture, customs, beliefs). At the same time, they discover mutual ground, which is the world of feelings and emotions, how we conduct our relationships, how we deal with our fears and problems, and how we express our sadness and joy.

Simultaneously, participants celebrate their miraculous diversity and potential. As troubadours of a new peaceful age, it is their intent to spread the wisdom, insights and loving attitude acquired during this process. If participants SPECIFICALLY INTEND to represent 1% of the global population, then their personal work on themselves will also positively affect this 1%, working through the morphogenetic field.

The vision of the Spiritual Revolution Project is that these seminars and processes take place worldwide and that participants from many countries built up partnerships with each other. Participants are also invited to search for their chosen "global villager" in real life, and to record their experience in articles / film / photographs as part of the project 100 SEEK 100.

PROJECT: ARTISTS CREATE PEACE

"The arts are not simply for amusement, distraction, representation or financial investment. They are a form of worship or service capable of awakening spiritual faculties and perspectives. We pledge to further the ARTS as A SACRED ACT WHERE EVERY BRUSHSTROKE AND TUNE AND MOVEMENT CAN BE CONDUCTED AS A PRAYER WHICH BLESSES AND ACCELERATES OUR JOURNEY TOWARDS PARADISE"

(From *The Artists' Manifesto*, Rosie Jackson)